ISBN 978-1-332-10123-8
PIBN 10284741

FB &c Ltd, Dalton House, 60 Windsor Avenue, London, SW19 2RR.
Company number 08720141. Registered in England and Wales.

For support please visit www.forgottenbooks.com

Antiquities of Bristow

IN THE

Middle Centuries;

INCLUDING

THE TOPOGRAPHY

BY

AND

THE LIFE OF

William Canynges,

BY

THE REV. JAMES DALLAWAY.

Bristol:
MIRROR OFFICE.
1834.

TO

GEORGE WEARE BRAIKENRIDGE, Esq.,

F.S.A. and F.G.S.,

Of Broomwell House, Brislington.

My dear Sir,

Added to claims of friendship, you have those of my approbation, for your singular perseverance in perpetuating the memorials of our native city.

Allow me, then, to offer this small volume under your patronage; which contains chiefly the Itinerary, as far as it relates to Bristol, made in the close of the fifteenth century, by the venerable WILLIAM WYRCESTRE, the earliest of our topographers.

The many localities now totally superseded, which he has marked out in description, you have identified in their several remains, with a liberal encouragement of competent artists, by no less than 1544 accurate drawings.

Your highly embellished library is still more distinguished by so rare and excellent a collection. It has been my grateful task to endeavour to smooth the ruggedness of my very ancient author; and to induce a perusal of him, by a partial translation of his desultory memoranda, as well as by explanatory notes. And it should be considered, that this singular MS. consisted of memoranda only, and those preparatory to a perfect work.

The Essay on Canynges and his times, is the result of more investigation of his personal history, than was previously known.

I am, my dear Sir,

With truth and regard,

Your faithful Friend and Servant,

JAMES DALLAWAY.

Letherhead, Surrey,

February 20th, 1834.

The ANTIQUARIES of BRISTOL may be gratified by a more detailed account of Mr. BRAIKENRIDGE's Collection of Drawings.

Of subjects in the Parish of St. Ewin's there are	44
All Saints	17
St. Werburgh's	34
St. John's	66
St. Stephen's	32
Christ Church	42
St. Peter's	69
St. Philip's	48
St. Nicholas	113
St. Mary Redcliff	126
Temple	70
St. Thomas	28
St. James	67
St. Michael	36
Castle Precincts	13
St. Leonard's	11
St. Paul's	7
St. Mary Le Port	17
St. Augustine	30
St. Mark's	69
Cathedral	160
Miscellaneous Drawings relating to Bristol	34
The Bridges and course of the River Froome	52
River Avon	74
Coloured Drawings of ditto	96
Vicinity of Bristol	54
Of Brislington only	135
Total number	1544

ERRATA.

P. 27. The note is transferred from p. 120 of Nasmith's Edition of the Itinerary.

P. 45. For Villa *read* Villæ.

P. 62. For *officium* read *offertum*.

P. 106. For Lane *read* Loud, and dele the asterisk.

P. 134. For Jocobi *read* Jacobi.

P. 136. For Hartery *read* Harptree.

P. 152. For Johis *read* Johes.—Johannæ *read* Johanna.—quoram *read* quorum.

P. 153. For demiferunt *read* demiserunt.

AN ATTEMPT TO DESCRIBE

THE

FIRST COMMON SEAL

USED BY THE

Burgesses of Bristol.

FROM THE

ARCHAEOLOGIA,

VOL. XXI.

AN ATTEMPT TO DESCRIBE

THE FIRST COMMON SEAL

USED BY THE

BURGESSES OF BRISTOL.

The first municipal Seal now extant, which was used by the commonalty of the burgh of Bristol, is no less curious for the excellence of the engraving as a work of art at the time of its execution, than the historical design, concerning which, I submit some Observations which have occurred upon a careful examination of it.

I have referred the adaptation of this design to a single event in the history of Bristol, of importance enough, as I would suggest, to have been thus commemorated; when the privilege of using a Seal was first conceded to the burgesses, by King Edward the First, as lord of the castle, in the early part of his reign.

Upon an inspection of the more ancient Borough Seals, I believe that it will be found, that the device of a castle is peculiar in a great degree, to those which were under the jurisdiction of a feudal lord, from whom they derived all their municipal privileges, and that the representation of a castle was retained upon those seals as evidence of their original dependance, long after their liberties were confirmed.

The seal under consideration is circular, having a diameter not exceeding three inches, cast in a composed metal, the basis of which is brass, and very skilfully intagliated or engraven. The Device is a Castle, having a high portal, or gateway, inserted between four towers rising from the banks of a river, and surrounded by a wall. The tower on the left hand is considerably larger than the others, intended to represent the keep. It has three tiers of circular arches; that on the right hand does not exceed half the dimensions of the keep, upon the top of which is placed a warder blowing a trumpet: the other two are low and diminutive. Of the great gateway, the arch is circular, and the door of timber frame has ornamented hinges of iron, but there is nothing to mark a portcullis. I have given a more minute description, because I have good reason to think that a representation of the castle of Bristol, as extant when the seal was made, was purposely intended. The earliest Seal of the city of Norwich bears a similar resemblance to its contemporary castle. The legend is engraven in the Lombardic character, "SIGILLVM. COMMVNE. BYRGENSIVM. BRISTOLLIE." But the obverse is the immediate subject of this disquisition. This is doubtless an equally exact representation of the other great gate of the ancient castle, which rose, flanked by towers, above the ditch into which the river Avon was admitted, and by which means, upon any disagreement with the burgesses, their maritime vessels might be seized and impounded. At the end of a wall is a lofty circular arch, having a high embattling or embrasure, upon which stands a man with his arm held out, and as if beckoning with his forefinger to a ship or large vessel rigged with a single mast and sail, and a pilot steering it with a rudder projected from the side,[a] rather resembling a broad plank, than the rudder of later usage. A similar form may be traced in the earliest delineations of the Norman æra.

[a] The most ancient rudder by which the ship was guided, in the time of the Romans is called by Virgil "*clavus,*" (in distinction from "*remus,*") and was attached to the side of the ship.

"Ipse sedens *clavumque* regit, velisque ministrat."
Æn. l. x. 218.

And in the 9th plate of the Bayeaux tapestry (published in the Archaeologia) the pilot holds the rudder in one hand, and the sail in the other. Upon the Trajan column, the clavus appears to have been likewise attached to the side of ships, and it is probable, that this usage prevailed during the whole period of the Roman empire, and that it was transmitted by them to the conquered provinces. That the Normans adopted the form and place of the rudder from them, the Bayeaux tapestry affords us several instances, with some variation, indeed, in its lower part. See plates i. ii. vi. vii. viii. ix. And in illuminations of a M.S. of Henry Knighton. C. C. Coll. Oxon. D. 4. f. 5.

Legend: X. SЄCRЄTI. CLAVIS. SV̄. PORT'.
NAVITA. NAVIS
[b]PORTA'. CVSTODIT. PORT'. VIĽIL.
INDICЄ. PDIT.

"Secreti clavis sum portûs. Navita navis
Portam custodit. Portum vigil indice prodit."

"I am the key of the secret port. The pilot steers the helm of the ship. The warder points out the port, with his fore-finger." The arch-way and tower are intended to represent the secret port large enough to admit vessels of considerable size, as an inlet or slip, immediately communicating with the larger or common port of the town, and occasionally serving the purposes of protection or annoyance.

To whatever circumstance this device, evidently historical, may indisputably owe its origin, it was certainly the prototype of all the City Seals, how-

[b] "Portam navis" is translated *(meo periculo)* at the steerage or helm of the ship, for I am unable to adduce any instance of its having been so used either in classic or monkish latinity. Such a pleonasm as "navita navis" can scarcely have been intended, and it was not the fact that the pilot kept the gate *(of the castle.)* The play upon the words "*porta* and *portus*" was too delightful to have been rejected by a rhyming monk; and he therefore used the former in a sense for which he had no authority. In the 14th century the *clavus* above mentioned appears to have been superseded by a rudder affixed to the stern, more resembling those of modern usage, and as may be seen in one of the illuminations of the Froissart, in the British Museum, like one half of folding gates, turning upon a hinge.

ever varied (as the building of the castle itself varied) in their mode of describing the circumstance: and likewise of the Arms of the City.

There are strong coincidences by which I am confirmed in an opinion, that the following event, which took place in 1275, gave occasion for this representation. This seal was used jointly for public acts, and for deeds issued by individual burgesses.

The first mention I have seen of a common seal of the burgesses, is in the charter granted them by King Edward III. in the 47th year of his reign, 1373, for the choice of a sheriff. "Sub sigillo communi dictæ ville Bristol;" but this circumstance does not prove that the common seal was then first made, but rather, that it had been previously extant.

I will now subjoin the historical fact, as related by the chroniclers of that age.

A large ship, which, by stress of weather, had been driven about in the British channel, was discovered, when becalmed, *(expansis velis)* hovering at the mouth of the Avon, by some pilots *(cives* not *nautæ)*. Walsingham says only four, who were in small boats. The ship excited the greatest astonishment, both from its size and furniture, and the certainty that persons of great consequence were on board. The *cives* (pilots) induced them, by promises of safety, to enter the harbour of Bristol, for it was not possible that they could have compelled them by actual force. Wykes, it is true, says "*puppim ipsam cum totâ sarcinâ capientes, invitos perduxerunt, intrinsecus,*" (into the creek and water-gate of the castle,) that is, after they had perceived that they had fallen into the hands of the enemy, and that all opposition would be useless. But Speed, from T. Walsingham, says only, that they were surprised.

Almeric de Mountfort had taken his sister, the daughter of the great Simon Earl of Leicester, (slain at the battle of Evesham,) accompanied by certain ladies, knights, and priests, with an intention of landing her on the Welsh coasts, and giving her in marriage to Leoline, or Llewellin, Prince of North Wales, who was then at war with King Edward the First. The treachery, or successful manœuvre, was the piloting of this ship, carrying, possibly, the marriage portion of the bride, with other splendid furniture, into the creek or *secret port* of the castle, instead of the *open port* of the town; and there surrendering the prize into the hands of the king himself, who, it may be inferred, was at that time keeping his court within his castle of Bristol.

The lady was treated with the courtesy, and the men with the savage barbarity, peculiar to that æra. Wykes relates that these "*cives*" of Bristol gave "*prædam ipsam non ignobilem Domino Regi, triumphali lætitiâ*;" and it is borne out by these circumstances, that the device or delineation of this achievement was represented upon the common seal of this burgh and port, and a superscription was added in monkish Leonine verse, obscure in itself, excepting that it be allowed to allude to this historical fact in particular; and it was then, first of all, confirmed by the royal authority.

In Peter Langtoft's Chronicle,[c] Almerike de Montfort is said to have been condemned by the parliament, held at Northampton. The whole family of Simon de Montfort had effected their escape into France. He gives an account of the transaction above alluded to, with a certain variation of some of its circumstances; but those are not less applicable to the device of this seal. A metaphrase may be more convenient for the present purpose; the original being subjoined in a note.[d]

"In the year after King Edward's coronation, Llewellyn Prince of North Wales sent into France to offer marriage to the daughter of Simon de Montfort, to which proposal her friends consented. And as they were now sailing or rowing towards

c "Almerike ov Montfort deprived was þere
And þe tressure that he had in kepyng."
Edit. Hearne, p. 222.

d "The next ȝere followand of Edward coronment;
Leulyn of Walsland, into France he sent
Ðe Montforts doughter to wedde, her frendes all consent,
Almirike her ledde to schyp, now ere hir went
Now they sail and row to Wales to Lewellynes,
A burgeys of Bristowe chargyd was with wines
He overtoke þere schyp, wiþens hir were?
Hii said wið King Philipp to Wales wold hir fare.
What dud þis burȝeys? disturbed his wendinȝ,
Ðe may and hir hernesse did lede unto ðe king;
Ðe mayden Edwarde toke, als he was full courteis,
In safety did hir loke and thankid þe burgeys.
Whan Lewlyne hard say to warre sone he began,
For tene he wend to die, þat taken was his leman."
Edit. ut sup. v.

Wales, to Llewellyn, Almerick her brother having her under his protection, a certain burgess of Bristol, who was in a vessel laden with wines, overtook the ship and demanded who they were? they answered that they were going with King Philip into Wales. What did this burgess? He misdirected their voyage by a stratagem, and took the maid and all her wedding furniture to King Edward. The maid the king took, and confined her for security, treating her with courtesy, for he was himself very courteous. The burgess he thanked and rewarded. When Llewellyn was informed of this event he prepared for war, for he was vexed mortally at the detention of his bride."

Trivetus, in his account of the place where Leoline's ship was first discovered and detained, is evidently mistaken. It was near a small island called Silley, on the Glamorganshire coast, and not the rock, better known by the same name at the land's-end, Cornwall.[e]

Elenor de Montfort was born in England and educated in France, married to Prince Leoline at Worcester, upon his pacification with Edward I. in 1278, " et anno sequenti mortua est."[f]

Such is the historical fact upon which I would ground my opinion, that it supplied the subject of

[e] " Comitissa de Leicester, vidua Simonis de Montfort, filiam suam transmisit in Walliam Principi maritandam; qui suspectum iter habentes per Angliam immenso multi maris spatio, ad insulas Iduras (quæ terminos Cornubiæ respiciunt) devehuntur." p 248. Seyer's Mem. of Bristol, vol. ii. p. 70.

[f] Ex registro Abbat. de Kainsham.

the obverse of the Great Seal of the Burgh of Bristol, which, from the circumstance of its castle having been both a garrison and a royal palace, was considered during the first Norman centuries as the metropolis of the West of England. The usage of the Lombardic character in all inscriptions for a great part of the thirteenth and the first years of the fourteenth century,[g] will fix the true æra of the seal under discussion, to 1275; when Edward the First, being resident in his castle of Bristow, and having there received so acceptable a prize "triumphali lætitiâ," it was very probable that he allowed an event, and the service so performed by the men of Bristow, to be commemorated upon their Common Seal as a royal boon or indulgence.

It is expressly said by Langtoft, that "he ðankede þe burȝeys;" and it might have been by this recognition. The royal, baronial, ecclesiastical, and municipal seals of this æra, are most of them executed with extraordinary skill and care, as to architectural representation, though those of men are beyond proportion, in this, as well as in other instances.

As I have been politely favoured with impressions in wax, taken from the ancient Seals now preserved in the archives of the city, by E. Ludlow, Esq., Serjeant at Law, the present Town

[g] The last Great Seal of England, the legend of which is inscribed in the Lombardic character, is that of Edward the Third, first used upon his claim of the crown of France, in 1338.

Clerk, I am greatly obliged to him for the opportunity of attempting a description of them, as a continuation of the former subject.[h]

II. This seal, which bears the full face and bust of a king crowned, crossed by a lion passant at the breast, and with a castellet on either side, is known from the legend to have been first issued by Edward I. It is likewise in the Lombardic character; "S. EDW. REL. ANL. AD. RECOLN. DEBITOR' AP'D. BRISTOLL." That the two castles are affixed, is an undoubted evidence that the first Edward is meaned, because they appear so placed upon his Great Seal, with reference to his Queen Elinor of Castile, as also upon several others.

III. This smaller seal, an impression from which is affixed to a deed in 1352, is inscribed: "SILILLVM. MAIORITATIS. VILLE. BRISTOLLIE," and was confined to the use of the Mayor and Sheriffs. It is a variation from the original already described, retaining the design.[i]

[h] These are engraved in Seyer's Memoirs of Bristol, vol. 1. p. 378.

[i] In Vincent's Collection of Drawings from Seals (MSS. Coll. Arm. No. 88. p. 42.) there is a later variety, in which the quarter for France has only the three fleurs-de-lys adopted by King Henry the Fifth, and the beacon is omitted. The legend is "Sigillum Majoritatis ville de Bristoll." It is affixed to the following deed. "Ego Thomas Halleway de Bristollia concessi tenementum, &c. Et quia sigillum meum quam plurimis est incognitum sigillum majoritatis ville Bristoll apponi. Dat. 10 Henrici 6ti 1432." Thomas Halleway was Mayor 1434, and founded a Chantry in the parish church of All Saints, with a com-

The ship has so far entered into the water-gate of the castle as to conceal its mast and sail. Upon the prow is displayed a pennon, large in proportion, bearing the arms of France and England quarterly, as they were first borne by King Edward III. and the Gothic letter 𝔅 behind it. The water-gate only of the castle, not the keep as in the former instance, is represented, and there are two warders with trumpets instead of one. On the highest turret there is a beacon, and near it a vane, upon which is a fleur-de-lys. The castle is no longer delineated as a Norman fortress; but the towers, which are lofty and slender, attached to the angles, have deep machicolations as introduced in the middle centuries after the Conquest.

IV. Is a Seal of small dimensions. Within a circle, covered with fleur-de-lys, is a leopard's face open-mouthed, with the tongue depending, and very deeply engraven. Legend; "S. MAIOR. STAPVLE. BRIST." Bristol was one of the seven staple towns in England, confirmed by King Edward the Third, in 1354, 27th of his reign, by whom it was enacted, in each of these towns, a seal should be kept by a distinct officer, styled the Mayor of the Staple.

petent endowment, in 1450. This is one only of very frequent instances of such an usage, for which the consent of the Mayor was previously obtained, upon petition. In a deed of Lucia Turteye 1350, "Et quia sigillum meum &c. ad rogatum meum specialem et personalem, Sig. Majoris villæ Bristoll, presentibus est appensum. Many of the curious deeds collected by the late Mr. Seyer and Mr. G. Cumberland, exhibit impressions of these several seals.

A question may arise, whether the architectural delineations of churches or castles engraven upon Seals are mere inventions, or in some instances accurate representations of buildings at the time they were made? I submit my opinion, that an analogy to the prevailing style was always intended. Conventual seals, upon which a church is the device, cannot perhaps be proved to represent accurately, that of the Convent to which they belong, as in the instance of that of St. Augustine, Bristol, yet the arches are circular, as were those of Fitz-harding's edifice. Upon a minute examination of the series of Royal Seals, from the Conqueror to King Henry VII. it will be seen that the architecture or shrine work of the thrones upon which each monarch is sitting, is at first composed of simple round arches, and that they then follow the style of the Gothic architecture, even to its final exuberance, in niches and canopies. It may be said, that they did not describe the precise form of any contemporary building, but that they sufficiently demonstrate the style.

We have still an opportunity of comparing the Castle of Norwich with the representation of one upon the Seal of that city, and shall find them analogous, in all respects, if not exactly resemblant. This reasoning may be applied to the more ancient Bristol Seal, as far as it relates to the general form of its castle, and more particularly of the water-gateway above the Avon.

As perspective or proportion were equally beyond the powers or conception of the graphic artists of that æra, we must be satisfied with a general idea only of all they intended to represent, and conclude that they described to the extent of their talents the transaction before mentioned, omitting none of the chief circumstances which if not of national were of local importance, as belonging exclusively to the History of the City of Bristol.

J. D.

Itinerarium,

SIVE

LIBER RERUM MEMORABILIUM

WILLELMI BOTONER

DICT. DE WORCESTRE.

E codicibus MSS. in bibliothecá C. C. C. Cantab. asservatis primus eruit ediditque,

Jacobus Nasmith ejusd. Coll. nuper Socius.

Notulas addidit, cum indice,

Jac: Dallaway. 1822.

What mannere Man he was—perchaunce,

Ye may behold the vraisemblaunce.

W. Botoner, *called* Wyrcestre.

PRELIMINARY OBSERVATIONS.

William Wyrcestre was the son of a person of the same name, who was a worthy burgess of Bristol, and engaged in trade. He was born at a house in a street called Saint James's Bec, in 1415. His mother was Elizabeth Botoner, of an opulent family settled at Coventry; by two rich individuals of which, the sumptuous church of the Holy Trinity in that city was erected, upon the authority of Dugdale, who describes their arms,—" Argent on a cheveron gules, three bezants, between three lions' heads erased and crowned, or." After having passed four years as a student of Hart-hall, in Oxford, he became a retainer to Sir John Fastolf, of Caistre Castle, in Norfolk, and, in process of time, his secretary, physician, and finally his executor. In the *Paston* letters, published by *Sir John Fenn*, in 1787, vols. 1, 3, and 4, there are several from him, respecting his employments, and the affairs of his executorship, and of the siege of Caistre Castle by John Mowbray, Duke of Norfolk. He then assumed the designation of W. Botoner, called Wyrcestre, preferring his mother's name to that of his father.

In the decline of life he established himself in Bristol, having a house and garden near St. Philip's church-yard gate, and various other property, " tria gardina W. W." There he cultivated medicinal herbs, and practised physic. His chief amusement in his old age was most minutely to survey his native town by paces and measurement, and committing the result of such investigation, daily, to his note-book. This circumstance will account for the desultory manner in which the MS. we are now examining is compiled and written. There is evidence collected from his notes, that he died about the year 1484.

He so frequently mentions the individuals of his family, that the following sketch of his descent may be considered to be proved :—

Botoner, *otherwise* **Wyrcestre.**

Argent on a cheveron between 3 lions' heads erased, gules, crowned or, 3 bezants.

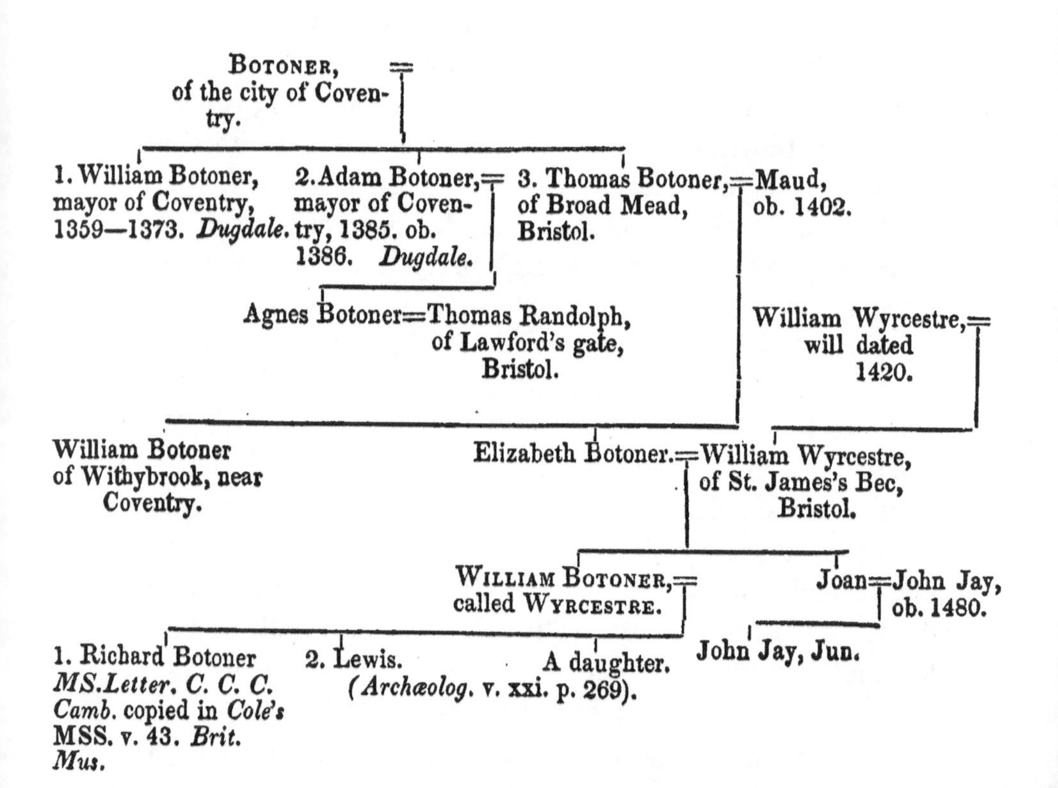

In order to fix local reference, the following Table is given from WYRCESTRE's Survey of BRISTOW, 1470—1480.

Points.	Streets.	Churches.	Convents, Chapels, and Hospitals.
E. from the High Cross.	Wynch-street (now *Wine-street*).		
	Mary Port.	St. Mary in Foro, or Le Port.	
	Peter (formerly *Castle-street*).	St. Peter.	
	Defence-lane.		
S.E.	Castle-street *(on the site of the Castle)*.		
	The old (or Castle) Market.		Barstaple's Hospital, Lawford's Gate.
	King's-street		
N.E.	The Pithay	St. James the Great.	The Franciscans.
	Broad-mead		The Gray Friars.
	Lewyn's-mead.		The Dominicans.
	St. James's Back *(or Bec, on the banks of the Froome)*.		
	——— Church-yard		
	——— Barton		
	The Castle *(Suburban)*.		The Benedictine cell to the abbey of Tewkesbury.
	Parish of St. Philip, and James the Less.	St. Philip and James the Less.	
W.	The Tholshyll.	All Saints.	The Calendars.
	Corn-street	St. Werburga.	
	St. Leonard's, with the Lanes.	St. Leonard (destructa).	
	St. Augustine the Less *(Suburban)*.	St. Laurence (destructa).	Abbey of Canons of St. Augustine (now the Cathedral)
	St. Augustine's Bec *(on the banks of the Canal)*		The Gaunt's Hospital.
S.W.	High-street, or St. Nicholas-street.	St. Nicholas.	
	Baldwyn-street.		
	Baft-street		
	March-street.		
	The Welsh Bec.		
N.W.	Small-street	St. Giles (destructa).	
	St. Leonard's } St. Stephen's } Lanes.	St. Stephen.	Carmelites.
N.	Broad-Street.	Holy Trinity, or Christ-church.	Chapel of St. George.
	The Quay.	St. Audoen (destructa).	

Points.	Streets.	Churches.	Convents, Chapels, and Hospitals.
		St. John.	
	St. Michael (*Suburban*).	St. Michael	Nunnery of St. Mary Magdalene.
N.E.	Tower-lane.		
N.W.	Hore-street (now *Horse-street*).		
	Knifesmith-street (now *Christmas-street*.		Hospital of St. Bartholomew.
S.	High-street.		St. Mary's Chapel on the bridge.
	The Bridge.		Knap's Chapel of St. John.
	St. Thomas-street.	St. Thomas.	
S.E.	Mary Port-street	St. Mary in Foro, or Le Port.	
	Worscep-street and Bocherew (now *Bridge-street.*)		
	Defence-lane.		
	Temple-stieet.	Temple, or Holy Cross.	
	Tucker-street.		Augustine Friars.
S W.	Redcliffe-street (*Suburban*).	St. Mary Redcliffe.	

The discrepancy complained of, which frequently occurs in William Wyrcestre's measurements, may be best examined by the collation of a single building; and therefore I select the Avon bridge, which is described with the greatest variation, and of which eight several mensurations are given in different parts of his MS.

So great a difference as that between 184 steps and 94 steps (*gradûs meos* each exceeding 20 inches) may be accounted for, by concluding that he measured from St. Nicholas church to Redcliff-street. We know that he used the half eight for the Arabic 4, which will reduce 184 to 144. The rise and fall on either side the bridge is included, so that the 94 steps, 150 feet (which measure is twice repeated) was exactly the length of the bridge, from the extremities of the stone piers between the gates. Another measure which he gives, of 72 yards (216 feet), may not be in fact contradictory, but depend upon the precise point beyond the stone work from which Wyrcestre began to measure.

The width between the houses upon the bridge is five yards, as he states, (once as nine steps, which at 20 inches make five yards), and ten yards, five on either side, to the outside walls of the houses, which were extended upon scantlings, placed upon the piers, and projected from them.

In his measurement of the chapel on the bridge there appears to be some contradiction. Forty steps is the external measure, and thirty the internal. Twenty-five yards is the length of the whole building, which rested upon piers, in the river, and crossed the street on the bridge.

Corrected readings are necessary to make any sense of some of William Wyrcestre's sentences; "pons pontis" should be "frons frontis," which Nasmith has mistaken. There were never two bridges over the Avon.

His own account of measures is satisfactory.

"26 gradûs i.e. passus. 5 palmæ, computando á pollice ad extremum punctum medii digiti.

60 steppys meos quæ sunt 84 virgæ.

24 steppys sive gressûs mei, faciunt 12 virgas.

50 virgæ faciunt 85 steppys.

5 virgæ sive 8 gressûs."

Here then is a positive statement.

It may be presumed that Barrett's measurements, actually taken for his History of Bristol, have a claim to accuracy. The subjoined is a fair comparison of the *Collegiate church of the Gaunts*:—

William Wyrcestre.	F	I.	*Barrett.* F.
Total length of the nave	71	8	72
Nave only to the end of the South aisle			51-123 ft. in all, by 24½ wide and 37 high; South aisle 72 ft. by 14½.

and of the *Holy Cross or Temple.*

William Wyrcestre.	YARDS.	*Barrett.*
Total internal length	57	Total length 156 ft. by 59
Square of the Tower	5	wide and 50 high.
	—	Nave 82 } 156
	62	Chancel 74 }
	—	

Is the discrepancy in these measures so great as to disparage Wyrcestre's general authority?

Upon an average, the "gressus" or pace will be found to be two thirds of a yard. "Brachia, vethym or fathom," six feet each.

In *Nasmith's* "Prefatio" are collected certain notices of William Botoner, called Wyrcestre.

"Itinerarium, sive liber memorabilium William Wyrcestre script. in viaggio de Bristol, usque ad montem S. Mich. in anno M.C.C.C.C.LXXVIII."

Notabilia Villæ Bristoliæ. *MSS. C. C. C. Cantab. Miscell.* M. "quod fere omnia continet, quæ habentur in autographo alio, in folio, formâ oblongâ, manu valde deformi, exarato," which is the genuine note-book of William Wyrcestre.

There is another MS. somewhat different, as including more, in the Lambeth library. *MSS. Wharton* L. p. 107.

Archbishop Parker procured a copy to be made from the original MS. in C. C. C. library, which Nasmith condemns, as being inaccurate.

The late indefatigable Cambridge antiquary, W. Cole, began to transcribe the original, but left it incomplete; it is to be found among the numerous volumes of compilations, which he bequeathed to the British Museum. *MSS. Cole.* vol. 42.

He observes, that however Mr. Nasmith may conceive that he has done justice to his author by omitting many curious particulars, by this caution in his preface "omnia quidem in editione nostrâ retinuimus, quæ ad historiam vel topographiam pertinent, sive majoris sive minoris momenti, cætera omittenda duximus." I do not well know how he can escape censure, which he has thus passed on the copy of this MS., which was taken by order of Archbishop Parker. "Habetur in hâc bibliothecâ apographum hujus codicis, sed *parum fidele*."

Cole has extracted

Page 35. *Additions.* "Expensûs a Bristoll a die mercurii usq. ad diem Nativ. B. M. Virginis 8 die Septemb. et usq. Tynterne per ij dies. Item pro candelo ceræ 2d—pro 9 billets de la Forest 8d. pro butyro ob. pro vino et repastis 3d.—pro equorum præbend. 9d. pro ferruâ 9d. pro reparatione sellæ 9d. pro medicina equi 2d. Summa 3 sol. 11d. Apud Welles cænandi, in toto, cum præbend: equorum 8d. ob. Apud Glastonbury in prebend: et repast: Item in pranditione per viam de Bristoll usque ad Glastynbury, 2 sol. 2d."

This extract, it must be allowed, is curious merely upon account of the prices he paid for the necessaries of his journey.

The pretensions of W. W. to learning, as it was professed among the few erudite ecclesiastics, may be subject to several considerations of abatement. But his love of learning was at all times superior to his acquirements, and his industry in copying many MSS., is sufficiently proved by those which are still extant. Nor can we say, concerning those which treat of science only, that he did not, in some degree, make them his own. As to his historical collections, and the memoranda which he made of what was passing in his own times, he must, in candour, be allowed all the merit which, in such times, was due to any lay-man, who dedicated his leisure to a literary pursuit. Several historical anecdotes of the reigns of Henry 5 and 6 are not to be found elsewhere, which came within his own knowledge.

The following catalogue is, I have reason to believe, more comprehensive and accurate than any already made.

From his habit of transcription, it is almost certain that he must have left many more MSS. Those which remain have been widely dispersed—yet it is certain that, as they are now preserved in celebrated libraries, they must have been held in considerable esteem.

Although these excerpts or selections do not entitle him to be considered as a man of deep learning, they will amply prove that he possessed an inquiring mind and great industry, especially as he was employed by his patron, Sir John Fastolfe, in the camp, in various negociations, and as seneschal or steward of his estates.

Twelve distinct MSS., some of which are voluminous, which may be still seen in different libraries, to which due reference is made in the annexed list, will afford sufficient proof that his diligence of transcription always seconded his opportunities. If we consider the general dispersion and frequent annihilation of such MSS. as are written upon paper, it is a matter of no small wonder that so many of them remain; and we may conclude that his industry in literary collections would have supplied many more, which have been destroyed.

May it not be candidly inquired—have not so many been preserved upon account of their intrinsic value?

MSS. of William Botoner, otherwise Wyrcestre, which are preserved in different Libraries.

1.—In Bibliothecâ Coll: Magdalen: Oxon. Gulielmi Vigorniensis de sacramentis scriptum 1473. Librum hunc Dno. Fundatori inscripsit Auctor.

2.—MSS. Cotton Julius F. vij, 5, W. Botoneri Registratio seu excerptio versuum, proverbiarum de Libro Ovidij de arte Amandi, de Fastis et de Epistolis A.D. 1462.

3.—MSS. Cotton, 504, p. 10. Catalogus illustrium Virorum, præcipue ecclesiasticorum scriptorum, à passione Christi usque ad ann. xiv. Theodosij, ex Diodoro Hispaliensi, Gennadio Massiliensi &c. excerpt. per W. W. Londini 1469.

4. MSS. 364. 5. Benet Coll: Cantab: De civitatibus, monasteriis, abatiis, &c.

5. Ejusdem. MS. 101. 221 pages. Codex chartaceus Henrici Principis Anglorum, Aristoxenus Musicus Oxoniensis doctissimus mense Maij 1474. Notæ de famosis actionibus illustrium virorum in quibusdam temporibus—mense Maij anno Xti. 1879 (1479.)

Ejusd. MS. p. 115. Excerpta de quodam libro Magistri Willelmi Plombe Collegij Gonvile Cantab. anno 1471 per me W. W. de Caistre. Vocalia Hebraica in latino exposita, habita in quodam Psalterio Hebraico, &c. scripta 20 die Augusti A. Xti. 1471. per W.W. Explicit Alphabetum in linguâ Hebraicâ de antiquo Psalterio Colleg: Sti. Petri Westmonasteriens: scriptum in linguâ et literis Hebraicis."

6. Mus: Catalog: Ayscough. N. 169. W.W. de ordinibus religiosorum tam nomine quam regulâ per W.W. de Bristolliâ in Diocesi Vigorniensi compilatis de diversis chronicis in civitate London, ad compilationem Dni. Nicholaj Ancrane, Prioris Sti. Leonardi prope Civitatem Norvic: 1464.

7. No. 179—Ejusd. De diversitate linguarum et grammatices secundum fratrem Ord. Francisi ad papam Clementem Quintum per W.W. Declaratio effectûs vere mathematica Rogeri Bacon.

8. MSS. Laud Bodleian Oxon. Tabulæ Alphonsi regis scripta, satis eleganter, per W.W.

9. Ejusd. MS. Stellæ versificatæ pro anno Xti. 1440, ad instantiam J. Fastolfe militis. Aliæ tabulæ pro eodem.

10. MSS. Soc: Antiq. London, No. 44. A paper volume in 4to., compiled by W. W., and addressed by his son to K. Edward 4th. A Collection of State Papers, chiefly relating to the regency of John Duke of Bedford, in France, Sir J. Fastolfe, &c., 22 articles. It is supposed to have been transcribed in the reign of Henry viij.

11. Brit: Mus: Catalogue MSS. Ayscough 4. 22. Receipts for catching fish.

Collection of divers receipts from several authors, both English and Latin, with a treatise called Dietarium Sanitatis custodiendæ, with several charms.

No. 17. Art. 26. Extracta Physicæ de libro Bertholi, de Johanne Greene Bristolliæ die Octobris 12: 1870 (1470.)

MSS. Coll. Arm. London. Lamentatio Regis Edwardi secundi (published by Hearne and Walpole.)

12. Biblioth. Lambeth MSS. De gestis Bedfordiæ Ebor. et Somerset Ducum. D. 6. Excerpta de eodem D. 85. pp. 91—107.

Dr. Chandler, in his life of *Waynflete,* relates Wyrcestre's conduct respecting the affairs of Sir J. Fastolfe, in his dispute with John Mowbray, Duke of Norfolk, and concerning the possession of the Castle of Caistre, as Sir J. Fastolfe's executor, in 1464.

W.W. gave to the library of Magdalene College, Oxford, a book intitled "De Sacramentis. Dedicationis sermo," which had belonged to Sir J. F. This MS. in 8vo. is still preserved there. Wyrcestre has inserted an account of his present and a date, 16 Dec., 1473. He had translated Cicero's treatises de Senectute et de amicitiâ, which he presented to Bishop Waynflete, and he complains that "se nullum regardum (*reward*) de Episcopo accepisse." Chandler observes that he probably obtained from the Bishop as much as it deserved. Yet, if his translation had been so imperfect, Caxton would scarcely have thought it worthy to be selected for his press. See Ames's History of Printing. Edit. Herbert. v. 1. p. 42.

This translation was undertaken by W. Wyrcestre by command of his patron Sir J. Fastolfe, not from the Latin but from the French version of Laurence Primierfaict.

THE

Topographical Account of Bristow

Commences at Page 166 of Nasmith's Edition of

THE ITINERARY OF WILLIAM WYRCESTRE.

Longitudo pontis Bristolliæ continet circa 72 virgas.

Latitudo ejus continet 5 virgas.

Sed tota latitudo cum mansionibus domorum scituatarum super pontem edificatarum continet . .

Longitudo capellæ Beatæ Mariæ, in medio pontis scituatæ continet 25 virgas.

Latitudo ejus continet 7 virgas.*

Longitudo vici le Bakk proxime continuati ab occidentali dictæ pontis, per longam keyam, coram aqua de Frome currit, continet in longitudine 220 gressus, vel tres 60 et 40 gressus.

Longitudo marisci ex parte murorum villæ propiendo a meridie ab extrema banci aquæ Avenæ prope le domum de rope-crafft vel latrinam officium, extendendo directe[a] *per calcetum* ad aquam de Frome

---

[a] "By the cause-way."

---

* Longitudo capellæ pontis Bristol continet 36 steppys. Latitudo capellæ prædictæ 12 steppys. *Itinerary*.

per [b]*rubeum calcetum* juxta muros villæ continet sic in longitudine dicti marisci videlicet sepcies 60 gressus, id est 420 gressus.

Longitudo viæ a porta Sancti Leonardi usque le key, transeundo per le custom-hous usque per le condyt, et directe per *shyppard hous*[c] velut via trianguli continet 90 gressus.

Longitudo viæ Baldewyne-strete tercies 60 et 30 gressus, 210 gressus.

Longitudo venellæ a porta Sancti Leonardi transeundo per cimiterium in Smalstrete 214 gressus.

Longitudo viæ vocatæ Seynt Laurens-lane a Smal-strete per Sanctum Laurencium 120 gressus.

Longitudo viæ de Smal-strete continet 240 gressus usque ad finem viæ ad portam Sancti Egidii ducentem ad unum vicum vocatum Seynt Laurens-lane.

Longitudo voltæ Sancti Johannis Baptistæ continet præter le chauncelle 29 virgas et dimidium.

Latitudo ejus continet 7 virgas.

Longitudo a cruce altâ eundo per vicum de Wynch-strete ad *le pilorye** faciunt 150 gressus. Et a le pyloire, continuando usque Newgate novies 60 id est 560 gressus. Et via de le Newgate ad pontem de le Were continet . . gressus.

Via de aqua de Weere eundo [d]*per fratres predi-*

---

[b] "Cause-way of red earth." [c] The house of J. Shipward, Mayor in 1477.
[d] The Convent of the Dominicans or Friars Preachers.

---

* The Collistrigium, or Pillory, was a high circular building of stone, upon the area of which this instrument of punishment, constructed with wood, was placed, so as to be always in public view.

catores et pontem ad finem viæ vocatæ Brodemede continet 224 gressus.

* Via a dicta fine viæ de Brodemede eundo per Marshalle-street† ad le barres ubi tenentes prisonei morantur de fatuis mulieribus continet . .

Longitudo cimiterii Sancti Jacobi Bristoll continet 150 gressus.

Latitudo ejus continet 100 gressus.

Latitudo navis ecclesiæ Sancti Nicholai inter vicum vocatum Sancti Nicholai ex parte boriali et vicum subteriorem ultra [e]*voltam vocatam introitus* ad le bakk, continet nisi 5 virgas.

Memorandum a porta turris vici Baldwyn-stret usque cornerium magnum in principio de le key per murum villæ sunt tres vices 60 id est 180 virgæ.

Item a porta Sancti Johannis eundo per Cristmas strete usque principium pontis portæ de Frome-yate sunt 124 gressus.

Longitudo pontis de Frome inter duas portas continet 24 gressus.

Item via de principio ultra et prope Newgate ad finem viæ ultra le Weere et le wateryng-place prope [f]*le graunt orchard* continet occies 60 et 20

---

e Called the Entrance Vault. f The great Orchard within the Castle walls.

---

* "Via a dictâ fine viæ de Brodemede ubi tenentes patris mei morantur ad les Barres de *fatuis mulieribus,* continet," &c. &c. *Cole's transcript. British Museum.* A curious distinction is afterwards made by W. W. between the first-mentioned and "*honestæ mulieres.*"

† *Marshalle-Street*—now corrupted to Merchant-Street, was so named from being the great military way, leading from the Castle, by which the garrison were marched

gressus id est 500 gressus, et Sanctæ Mariæ *de la port** continet nonies 60 et 20 gressus, id est 560 gressus.

Via prope ecclesiam Sancti Petri ducente de Wynch-strete ad principium cornerii viæ orientalis partis incepcionis de [g]*le bochery* continet ex transverso prope fontem de via prope ecclesiam Sancti Petri etc, continet . . gressus.

Via incipiente ex parte orientali de le bochery eundo per longitudinem viæ de [h]*lez shamlys* continuando ad finem portæ Sancti Nicholai continet in longitudine quinquies 60 et 34 gressus, id est 334 gressus.

---

[g] The Butcher-row, called likewise Worship-street, because the King's Custom-house was situate there, now Biidge-street. [h] "The Shambles."

---

towards the Mons acutus (Montacute) and King's down, for warlike exercise and sports.

The ground plan of *ancient Bristow* formed an irregular circle, and it is remarkable, that the four cross streets are not built in a regular line; every other circularly, one behind another, still following the outline of the Town walls.

THE SEVEN HILLS OF BRISTOL.

1 The Castle, central point.
2 St. James, N.E.
3 St. Michael, N.W.
4 St. Augustine, S.W.
5 St. Brendan, W.
6 St. Mary Redcliff, S.
7 Mons acutus / King's down. N.W.

* *Sanctæ Mariæ in Foro,* where was the market for the city. The market for the garrison in the castle was the "viel mercate" the Old Market. *St. Mary de la Port.* Port anciently meant the burgh or town. The common meadow near Oxford, which is free to the townsmen, is still called Port-meadow. And the lane under the town wall, in Redcliff-Street, is still called Port-Lane.

Longitudo de 4 domibus magnis de le bochery continet 25 gressus.

Latitudo 4 *domorum magnarum de bochery*[k] continet . . gressus.

Et subtus dictarum magnarum domorum sunt grossæ et magnæ voltæ.

Vicus qui incipit a prima parte pontis et fluminis de Radclyff-strete usque cornerium viæ incepcionis de Temple-strete apud *Stallage-crosse** continet sexies 60 id est 360 gressus, et finiens dicta via apud le slepe de Avyn in angulo viæ borealis transeundo per magnum fontem.

Via incepcionis apud le Avyn in parte boriali de Stallage-crosse, eundo per longam viam ad Temple-yate continet 110 gressus usque crucem vocatum Stallage-crosse; et continuando dictam viam de cruce prope ibidem vocata Stallage-crosse usque ecclesiam [l]*Crucis Sanctæ Templi* ecclesiæ predictæ continet 300 gressus; et sic continuando ad finem portæ vocatæ Temple-yate continet 320 gressus.

[m]*Porticûs Templi* longitudo continet 9 virgas; latitudo portæ templi continet 3 virgas.

Latitudo principii viæ Temple-strete ex parte boriali de Stallage-cros continet . . gressus.

Latitudo viæ in fine apud Temple-gate continet 20 gressus.

Temple-strete, vicus ultra portam templi versus

---

k The ancient Slaughter-houses and Flesh-market. l "Holy Cross, or Temple." m The Porch of Temple Church.

---

* Stallage or Market Cross stood in the midst of the market stalls, near Temple Church, belonging to the Knights Templars, for the supply of the tenants of their peculiar district.

ecclesiam Sancte Mariæ de Radclyff continet 420 gressus.

Latitudo viæ de le Temple-strete prope portas ecclesiæ [n]*fratrum Sancti Augustini* continet 20 gressus.

Domûs altissimæ et latæ regis cum voltis in vico de Worshyp-strete, alias shamellys, sive bocherye.

In vico vocato le shamelys sunt 3 profundissimi cellarii regis* sub tribus domibus magnæ et altæ edificaturæ, quæ fuerunt ordinatæ pro lanis et mercandisis custodiendis ad onerandas naves Bristolliæ ad exteras partes ultra-marinas. Et similiter sunt in dicto vico 4 alii cellarii.

Volta profundissima sive cellarium [o]*fortissimum* subtus portam Newgate.

Super pontem Bristoll. est pulcra volta larga, artificiose operata subtus capellam Beatæ Mariæ [p]*pro consulibus et juratis villæ Bristolliæ* sedendis, et ad conciliandum pro communi utilitate villæ.

Super dictum pontem Bristolliæ sunt 4 cellaria in fine et principio pontis.

Spacium super [q]*le Tolsylle,* ubi major et conciliarii villæ obviant de die in diem, quando videtur

---

n "The Hermits of St. Augustine." o "A Dungeon arched with stone."
p "For the Common Council and jurats of the town." q "The Tolsey."

---

* These very numerous and spacious cellars for the safe keeping of the heavier merchandise, as well for the King's customs, as the cargoes belonging to individual merchants, formed in fact the "subterranean Bristol." In some instances, a floor was made by large transverse beams of timber; in more, the vaults were of stone, pointed arch; rarely with ribs or other ornament.

expediens, sub [r]*coopertura de cyling cum plumbo*, coram [s]*hostium occidentale* ecclesiæ Christi continet 5 virgas ; et ex alia parte coram Hygh-strete continet . . virgas.

Officium domus conciliarii tam majoris, vicecomitis, ballivorum villæ ac conciliariorum principalium eorundem, tam de principalibus mercatoribus cum expediens fuerit, est scitum prope le Tolsyllecourt, est proxime sequens spacium apertum de stacione super le Tolsylle ex opposito cancellæ ecclesiæ Omnium Sanctorum,* cum cameris desuper honestissime preparatis pro conciliariis gubernatorum dictæ villæ annexis in parte meridionali ecclesiæ Sancti Adoeni.

Pyll-strete in parochia Sancti Stephani.†

Via a porta Sancti Leonardi, incipiente sub porta Sancti Leonardi, videlicet a fine viæ de Baldwynstrete, directe eundo per venellam conducentem ad le key Bristoll., ubi le custom hows in principio [t]*trianguli super le key*, qui quidem triangulus est in parte meridionali de le key, in medio cujus trianguli *excellens domus conducti* de frestone scita est et

---

[r] A ceiling covered with a flat roof of lead." [s] "The west door."
[t] The triangular open space on the Quay, where were the Custom-house, and the Castellet of a Fountain, now covered with warehouses. The fountain remains.

---

* The ancient site of the Tolsey had, like the present, one front opposite the west-door of Christ-church, and the other opposite the chancel of All Saints.

† There were two streets bearing nearly similar names ; Pyll street in St. Stephen's parish, and Pile-street, which branched from Redcliff-hill.

construitur; et dicta via modo est finis de la Pylle strete, continet 100 gressus.

Latitudo dictæ venellæ continet 5 virgas ad incepcionem anguli dicti trianguli de le custom-hows, et ibidem finiente.

[u]*Venella parvissima et stricta* eundo de Hyghstrete prope altam crucem inter ecclesiam omnium sanctorum et [w]*officium artis cocorum villæ*,* extendendo per cimeterium ejusdem ecclesiæ et meridionalem partem dictæ ecclesiæ juxta murum novæ alæ, edificatum diebus juventutis meæ per hostium meridionale ecclesiæ predictæ;† et juxta quem murum dominus Thomas Botoner presbiter fuit sepultus in parte orientali [x]*hostii* meridionalis, sed credo ossa dicti domini Thomæ sunt remota tempore edificationis novæ alæ, et tumba de frestone ejus similiter est remota; et dicta stricta venella in longitudine extendit ad parvam et curtam viam in occidentali parte dictæ ecclesiæ ad *finem hospitii alti*[y] prioris

---

[u] "A very small and narrow lane." [w] "The shops of the art or mystery of the Cooks of the Town." [x] "Door." [y] "The lofty dwelling-house."

---

* It appears from this and similar passages, that the artificers were supplied from cooks' shops, and not from domestic establishments. In King's street, there were likewise such shops for the supply of the soldiers of the Castle. There were many cook shops near the church and gate of St. Nicholas.

† This south aisle of All Saints'-church was rebuilt in the time of W. W.'s youth (about 1420) by the Calendaries, whose college was adjacent, and served for their chapel. In 1451, John Gyllard Prior died. He had expended £217 upon the library over the north-aisle, with a curious ceiling of carved oak, now taken down.

collegii vocati [z]*lez kalenders*, ubi dictus dominus Thomas Botoner fuit, ut supponitur, consocius, et in domo prioratûs hospicii obiit, ex certâ scientia Elizabet sororis suæ, matris meæ, michi relatæ, circa ætatem juventutis meæ quasi sex annorum ut suppono, quia quamvis fui presens secum die mortis suæ cum matre mea valefaciendo die ultimo vitæ suæ, non [a]*habui discrecionem ad noticiam personæ suæ;* et ut credo cartæ et evidenciæ tam hereditatis suæ in tenemento suo prope Yelde-hall in Bradstrete ex parte meridionali dictæ Gyldhall, necnon de hereditate ejus per Thomam Botoner patrem ejus et matris meæ in villa de Bokyngham, in Westrete jacentem versus aquam in parte . . scitam ac in villis adjacentibus de racione deberent remanere, quando queratur *de priore kalendarii** si remanent inter eorum evidencias

---

[z] The College of the Calendaries, or Public Registrars. [a] " I was too young to remark her person."

---

* The Prior and Confraternity of the Kalendaries of Bristol. " The Calendaries, otherwise caullid "the Gilde or Fraternitie of the clergy and commonaltie of Brightstow," was first kept in the church of the Trinitie, sens at All Hallows. The original of it, is time out of mynd."—*Leland Itin.* v. 7. p. 94.

Leland has " a remembraunce of memorable acts done in Brightstow, owt of a litle boke of the antiquities of the howse of Calendaries in Brightstow."—*Itin.* v. 7. p. 94.

John Harlow, Prior of the Kalendaries, and his brethren are mentioned in a charter dated *Rot. Pat.* 34 *Edw. 3tij.* p. 2. m. 13; and "Domus Calendariorum Bristol" was valued at the dissolution at £10. 18s. 8d. a year. The last

de evidenciis domini Thomæ Botoner consocii eorum.

Longitudo dictæ [b]*venellæ strictæ* continet 60 gressus.

Latitudo dictæ venellæ continet tres pedes sive unam virgam.

Via brevis de Corn-strete returnando per occidentalem partem hospicii prioris de kalenders continet in longitudine 170 gressus.

Latitudo viæ continet 5 virgas prope Corn-strete.

Cellarium unum, vel duo, [c]*pro vinis vendendis* est in dicta via parva.

. . . .

. . . .

circumgirata, quæ quidem venella alciora et ulteriora trium dictarum venellarum, quarum una incipit venella in medio vici vocato Horstrete ad angulum muri gardini fratrum carmelitarum ad *ymaginem Beatæ Mariæ in muro predicto scitam,** continuat usque crucem de lapide et fontem remo-

---

[b] "Narrow lane." [c] "Used by Vintners for selling wine by retail."

Prior was Thomas Sylke. Their office was to record all memorable matters, as they occurred in the Burgh.

Robert Ricart, a Calendar, who held the Town-clerkship, compiled a register (18 Edw. 4) 1478, which is a singularly curious M.S., now preserved among the City Archives. It is written upon vellum and paper, with several coloured delineations, but extremely rude.

* It was customary to place statues of the Virgin Mary at the angular parts of the streets, in great towns, in lofty niches, for the adoration of the people.

ciorem ad caput montis viæ de Stepe-strete; et venella secunda *incipit ad dictam fontem sive crucem,** et vocatur Frog-lane, et continuat in parte retro ortorum ecclesiæ de Gauntes et sanctuarium.

Venella in Horstrete juxta occidentalem partem ecclesiæ Sancti Bartholomei vocata Stype-strete, [d]*incipiendo et descendendo* ad ecclesiam Sancti Michaelis usque ad crucem et fontem de frestone continet . . .

Venella secunda in Horstrete incipiendo ad finem muri fratrum Carmelitarum, [e]*ubi ymago Sanctæ Mariæ ponitur in tabernaculo muri fratrum,* et transeundo versus montem Sancti Michaelis usque ad finem dictæ venellæ vocatæ . . . . continet . . gressus.

Via de inceptione dictæ venellæ in Horstrete ex dextra, viam eundo per murum fratrum ad introitum ecclesiæ fratrum continet coram le bak fratrum in opposito de le key Bristolliæ 80 gressus.

Venella alia ex sequenti via de Horstrete ad Sanctum Augustinum eundo, sed incipit ad portam introitus ecclesiæ fratrum Carmelitarum per viam de [f]*le bakk*, et sic eundo ad borialem plagam

---

[d]" Setting out and going down." [e]" Where the image of St. Mary is placed within a niche in the wall of the friar's garden." [f]" St. Augustine's Bec."

---

* Upon the summit of St. Michael's hill, called Stype or Steep Street, there was a cross of stone, which surmounted a covered well, for public accommodation. The lower part was called Stoney hill, immediately above the very spacious gardens which belonged to the Carmelite Priory.

per Froglane scindendo viam, et sic continuando dictam venellam borialiter ad finem dictæ venellæ continet 240 gressus versus montem Sancti Michaelis.

Venellæ super le key coram aqua de Frome currente de le key.

Prima venella super le key eundo ad Mersh-strete, incipiendo ad *domum principalem lapideam** inceptionis de le key versus le mersh ex opposito . . . continet 80 gressus.

Secunda venella sequens versus ecclesiam Sancti Stephani infra latitudinem viæ 30 gressuum, continet ejus longitudo 90 gressus.

Tertia venella de keya eundo ad ecclesiam Sancti Stephani [g]*per portam meridionalem novam ecclesiæ* usque ad finem ecclesiæ orientalem continet 180 gressus.

Quarta venella de le key eundo per alteram partem ecclesiæ Sancti Stephani per le north door usque le Mersh-strete continet 84 gressus.

Quinta venella eundo ab domo, incipiente coram portam meridionalem ex novo factam ecclesiæ, eundo novum campanile et [h]*costeram parietis borialis ecclesiæ* continet 90 gressus.

Sexta venella a loco trianguli de le key de domo

---

[g] "Before the South porch of the Church, then newly erected." 1480.
[h] "The side of the North wall of the Church."

---

* Large houses, built of stone, were then rare in Bristol.

magistri* Shyppard subtus celarium, sic eundo ad ecclesiam Sancti Stephani ex parte boriali usque ad . . . . . continet 90 gressus.

Triangulus vicus de le key in quo loco magni spatii dicti trianguli, ubi pulchrum conductum aquæ scitum est de frestone erectum pro commodo villæ, computando sive numerando ab angulo de vico vocato le key coram aquam de Frome, et eundo directâ viâ ad oppositum loci, viz versus

* The connection by intermarriages, between the families subsequently noticed, is remarkable. In several instances, one family has become the heirs-general of another.

Descent of SHIPWARD, *as proved from Deeds and Wills.*

Shipward.

Argent a cheveron between three anchors sable.

John Shipward=Katherine
Bailiff 1413.

John Shipward=Gwinett
Mayor 1453, Will proved 1473, Founder of St. Stephen's Tower.

John Shipward =
Mayor 1477. Completed the same

John Shipward. | Agnes=Edmund Westcote.
Isabel=John Norton, of Bristol.

cimeterium Sancti Leonardi, ubi incepcio [i]*solarii domorum edificatarum super trabes**, ita quod homo potest sicco pede transire per keyam ad ecclesiam Sancti Laurencii, continet 49 gressus.

De muro villæ circa le mersh et le key.

Murus villæ; longitudo videlicet a prima porta vocata le mersh-yate prope finem viæ de le bakk, ab aqua de Avyn sic transeundo per le mersh prope dictum murum, usque portam secundam villæ ad finem viæ de mersh-street continet in longitudine 440 gressus; et continuacio dicti muri vocati le towne-walle eundo de dicta porta secunda vocata le Mersh-yate, transeundo per locum ubi naves de novo sunt erectæ et compositæ, ac arbores et mastys de [j]*vyrre* cum anchoris jacent et cellarii plures et spacium magnum infra dictum murum usque primum angulum de le key Bristolliæ in occidentali parte de le key, ubi naves magnæ jacent in [k]*le woose* in parte occidentali de le key, eundo versus ecclesiam Sancti Stephani et ecclesiam Sancti Laurentii, continet longitudo dicti muri 320 gressus: et in toto dictus murus a prima porta de le bak usque eundem primum locum inceptionis pavimenti de le key, continet 760 gressus.

---

[i]Chambers of houses built upon transverse beams, under which was a cloister or covered way for the foot passengers. [j]"Fir timber." [k]"Mud or slough."

---

* This cloister or cóvered way was made beneath the upper floor of the houses, laid upon beams, like those called the "Rows," still remaining at Chester.

Altitudo dicti muri continet per estimationem 40 pedes.

Latitudo dicti muri continet 8 pedes.

Apud hygh-crosse 4 viæ quadriviales, videlicet, Hygh-strete, Bradstrete, Wynchstrete, et Seynt [l]*Collas*-strete.

At Seynt Collas yate in the north syde of the yate meten acrosse wyse IIII weyes, whych ben the shamelys and Seynt Nicholas strete, the waye entryng to the [m]*hogge*-yate, and the seyd Hygh-strete.

At the sout-side of Seynt Collas yate meten twey chyff weyes, the chieff brygge upon IIII grete arches of x vethym yn hyth, and the fayre chappelle upon the v arch, and the second way havyng the space of a tryangle goyng to bak by Seynt Nicholas chyrch.

Item at the begynnyng of the bakk, there the fyrst gryse called a slypp, ben twey weyes, the fyrst wey ys the seyd slepe of . . . yerdes long, goyng to the water called Avyn-water to wesh clothes, and to entre ynto the *vessels and shyppes that comen to the seyd bak*,* and the second way entryth yn Baldwyne-street.

---

[l] Nicholas. [m] Pig-market.

---

* "The haven by Avon flowithe about a two miles above Brightstow bridge. The ships of olde tyme cam only up by Avon to a place caullyd the Beck, wher was and is depthe enowghe of watar, but the bottom is very stony and rughe; sens by policye they trenched somewhat alofe by north weste of the olde key on Avon, anno 1247, and in

At the Crosse yn Baldwyne strete been IIII crosse wayes metyng, one waye goyng ys a grete wyde way goyng to Bafft-strete, the second waye goyng northward by a hygh grese called a steyr of XXXII steppys ynto Seynt Collas strete ; the other tweyn metyng wayes at the seyd cros of Baldwyne streete.

At the south syde of Seynt Johnys ys yate meten also IIII crosse weyes, whych one chief way ys Bradstrete, the second ys Toure-strete bye Seynt John ys chyrch goyng streyt too Wynch-streete, and ys bnt a streyt way goyng by the old towne walle and the old toune yate called blynd yate, streyt by the auntient fyrst yate called Pyttey-yate uppon the hylle entryng ynto Wynch-strete, called Castel-streete.

The III[d] wey ys Seynt Laurens-strete goyng from Seynt Johnys yate ynto Smalle-strete.

The IIII[d] way throw the seyd yate of Seynt John goyng ynto Cristmas-strete, called Knyf-smyth-strete.

In the north syde of Seynt Jonnys yate ys a III triangle ways, one way goyng right to Cristmasse-strete warde.

The second way goth [n]*rygh est* by the woult of Seynt Johnys chyrch, [o]*goynt* ynto *Gropecount-*

---

[n] Right east. [o] Immediately.

---

continuance bringing the course of Avon ryver that ways hath made a softe and wosy (oozy) harborow for grete shippes."—*Leland Itin.* v. vij. p. 89.

*lane** to Monken-brigge a pryson place some-tyme.

The III way goyng a crosse way to the kay by the lower way of Seynt Laurens, and by the old temple yewys where be grete vowtes under the hygest wallé of Bristow, and the old chyrch of Seynt Gylys was byldyd ovyr the vowtes yn the way goynt to Seynt Laurens laane ynto Smal strete.

At Seynt Leornard yate yn the east syde meten wythynne the yate IIII quadryvyalle weyes, as Corn-strete in the est parte, the second way toward the north ys Seynt Leonard way goyng from the chyrch streyt into Small-strete; the III way goth esterly from Seynt Leonard chyrch ynto Seynt Collas strete.

The yate of Seynt Leonard under the seyd chyrch crosseth II weys, the south-east way ys Baldwyne strete goyng to the bak; the secund way ys called Pylle strete, there of old dayes renne the water called Frome by Baldwyne-strete to the bakk, fallyng ynto Avyn-water,† and whych Pylle strete gooth streyt north by the old custom-house to the kay, where ys a grete space lyke to a large tryangle, and yn the myddel of the seyd triangle ys a fayre tour of frestone bylded.

* So mentioned in the description of the house of T. Lawrence, in a lease dated 12 Edw. 3tij. There were lanes so named in Oxford and Coventry.—*Leland.* So narrow that two persons could not pass through them abreast.

† When the Harbour was made in 1247, and the river Froome turned into it, the course behind the present Baldwyn street was filled up.

Item yn the myddys of Pyle-strete toward the new chyrch toure of Seynt Stevyns metyn IIII ways dyversly at the entree of Seynt Stevyns chyrch yerd at the style or lytille yate; the first way westward ys a large and a long way called Mersh-strete during to Mersh yate, there many merchauntes and also maryners duellin.*

At the seyd chyrch style ys a laane goyng yn the south syde of Seynt Stevyn chyrch, going by the chyrch yerde to the kay by old Leycetyr dore in the north syde of the toure of the chyrch by the new doore to the seyd kay.

Item at the eende of the seyd Pylle-strete by the seyd lane that retorned by the begynnyng of the seyd fyrst lane ys another laane, that goth evyn ryght by the este ende of Seynt Stevyn chyrch under the hygh auter, and so contynewyth the seyd laane to the seyd kay northly.

Item out of that laane that gooth by the est eende of Seynt Stevyn chyrch returnyth another laane from the north syde of Seynt Peter chyrch by the west dore of the seyd church, turnying to aforeseyd fyrst laane so entryng to the kay.

At New-yate, ubi quondam scola grammatica per magistrum *Robertum Lane*† principalem gram-

* Marsh Street contained many very capacious and curiously constructed houses of timber-frame; in which, from its contiguity to the Quay, the principal merchants of that age were induced to reside. No street in the city was, at that time, inhabited by more opulent merchants and mariners.

† Loud. See inscription in St. Peter's church.

maticum cum . . . . *Leland** magistro grammaticorum in Oxonia, dicebatur fuisse flos grammaticorum et poetarum temporibus annis plurimis revolutis, et tempore quo primum veni ad Oxoniam universitatem scolatizandi, obiit in termino paschæ anno Christi 1432 circa mensem junii, quando generalis eclipsis, die Sancti Botulphi, accidebat.

At the seyd New-yate yn the west part of yt wythynne Bristow there meten 11 large weys; and the norther way is called Towr-strete aliter Wynch-strete, and so goth by the old yate of the toune about 120 steppys yn length to the hygh crosse ward, where the olde towne walle stode.

Memorandum quod a principio franchesiæ de sanctuario Sancti Augustini abbathiæ, incipiendo ad metam cimiterii antiquæ ecclesiæ isto anno Christi 1480 noviter constructæ, eundo, per medium sanctuarii ad finem ejusdem, videlicet ad descensum terræ ad finem sanctuarii vocatum le west partye, per primum murum et viam domûs lapideæ in eadem parte viæ, eundo versus [p]*lymotes* ubi ecclesia de Gauntes habet introitum in ecclesiam predictam, continet 360 gressus.

Latitudo dictæ viæ eundo ad lymotes sub Brandon-hille continet 42 gressus.

Et a dicto angulo domus muri in orientali parte ecclesiæ [q]*de la gauntys* continet 720 gressus, videli-

---

[p] Limites Villa. [q] The Gaunt's, or St. Mark's Chapel.

---

* Laylond. "Ut Rosa florum, sic Laylond grammaticorum." His name was John.—See *Tanner's Bibliotheca.*

cet sub monte *Beati Brandani** ecclesiæ de Gauntes ex parte boriali sanctuarii Sancti Augustini in eundo ad mansionem versus villam Rownam et Ghyston-clyff vocat Lymotes, ubi lapis altus de freestone longitudinis unius virgæ sive trium pedum pro meta, limita five butta, quæ est ultimus finis libertatum et franchesiæ de villa Bristolliæ super aquas de Avyn et Severn currentes ad Rownam directe sub pede montis Sancti Brendani, continet a principio introitus sanctuarii usque dictam domum de Lymotes, hoc est intelligendo dictum introitum ad dictum sanctuarium Sancti Augustini computando ad *vetus* et primam ecclesiam dictæ abbathiæ, quæ modo est ecclesia parochialis noviter edificata, continet in toto 980 gressus.†

* "Here beginneth the life of St. Brendane," over a wooden cut of that saint, in full length, holding an open book in his left hand, and a croisier in his right, with *Caxton's* Cypher. It begins thus—"Seynte Brendane the holie man was a monk and borne in Ireland. And then he was Abbot of an hous, wherein were a thousand monks." Emprynted by *Wynkyn de Worde*. *Herbert's History of Printing*. V. 1., p. 220.

Upon the summit of Brandon-hill there stood anciently a chapel, to which the Irish mariners resorted upon their reaching the port of Bristol. Upon the same spot, during the Civil Wars, a bastion was erected connecting the Royal Fort with the river. No vestige now remains of either.

† Here Cole's transcript ends. The Itinerary was transcribed before Nasmith's publication, in part only, and not completely, by the Rev. William Cole, the celebrated Cambridge antiquary, who bequeathed many MS. volumes to the British Museum. It occurs in the 42d volume at the beginning. Upon collating it with the printed copy, I found very few variations, and those of no consideration.

Apud rupem altissimam de Ghyston-clyff, quæ incipit prope villam passagii de Rownam usque heremitagium et castellum in altera parte aquarum de Avyn et Frome, quæ rupis altissima incipit per unius miliaris spacium de villâ Bristolliæ, et continet dicta rupis in altitudine per longitudinem unius miliaris et ulterius versus Rownam-rode pro navibus reponendis, et dicta rupis continet in altitudine ab aqua de Avyn et Frome 60 brachia, videlicet de firma terra ad quoddam heremitagium, cujus ecclesia fundatur et dedicatur in honore Sancti Vincentii, sunt in altitudine 20 brachia, et a dicto heremitagio ad profundum aquarum predictarum sunt 40 brachia, et intellige quod brachium continet 6 pedes longitudinis.

Castellum super altitudinem terræ non distans per quartam partem miliaris de Ghyston-cliff, ut dicitur a vulgaribus plebeis, ibidem fore fundatum ante tempus Wilelmi conquestoris per Saracenos vel Judeos per quondam Ghyst gigantem in terrâ . . . . . . et quod tale castellum* verisimile erat antiquis temporibus fundatum remanet in hodiernum diem in magno circuitu congeries magnorum lapidum et parvorum sparsim seminatorum, valde mirabile visu dictos lapides ita globose jacentes in ordine et circuitu maximo, quod ibi videbatur fuisse castrum fortissimum, quod [r]*centenariis annis preteritis* fuisse dirutum et ad terram

---

[r] " many hundred years ago."

---

* Castellum evidently means the Roman Camp.

funditus prostratum, et ideo quod est decus et honor patriæ Bristoll. et comitatui Gloucestriæ habere vel audire fundaciones nobilium fortaliciorum et castrorum, hic inter alia scribo per modum memorandi de isto castro sive fortalicio.

Via trianguli a porta Sancti Nicholai usque le bak per principium pontis Bristoll.

Trianguli latitudo de angulo domus conducti aquæ de frestone in primo introitu ad le bak, eundo ad portam Sancti Nicholai contra Hyghstrete, et eundo [8]*per et prope* le croude continet 40 gressus.

Latitudo viæ ad dictum introitum de le bakk ad angulum cornerii proximi continue dictam domum de frestone* prope angulum strictum unius grocer ibidem in parte dextrâ continet 5 gressus.

Pars lati trianguli predicti eundo de le boteras in parte de le bocherew infra principium pontis usque ad supradictum angulum prope principium de le bakk prope dictam domum conducti aquarum continet 40 gressus.

Caput trianguli predicti de inceptione primæ partis pontis Bristolliæ ex parte sinistra usque

---

[8] "by and near."

---

* Houses constructed with freestone were rare in the ancient town. Many of timber frame were erected in the principal streets, which contained spacious rooms, a few of which still remain. They had projecting fronts upon large brackets, richly and curiously carved, and bay windows, with the intermediate space likewise filled with glass.

directe eundo ad angulum oppositum viæ latitudinis pontis predicti continet 20 gressus.

Latitudo viæ Touker-strete* ad finem pontis Bristoll. eundo versus Stallage-cros continet 14 gressus.

Latitudo viæ de Seynt Thomas strete strictè ad inceptionem et introitum viæ strictæ in longitudine circa 66 gressus continuando per murum longum, eundo continuè ad Seynt Thomas strete, continet illa latitudo 5 gressus; et sic continuando ad vicum Seynt Thomas strete et per domum quadratam de frestone pro aqua gentibus illius parochiæ et circum manentium usque ad murum villæ Bristolliæ retornando versus Radclyff-yate continet in longitudine 305 gressus.

Longitudo de Seynt Leonardes yate usque ad ecclesiam Sanctæ Werburgæ continet 120 gressus ad medium introitus ecclesiæ Sanctæ Werburgæ; et sic continuando per altam crucem continuè usque eundo per officium domus de le Pyllorye, continuando ad antiquissimam portam de le Oldgate muri villæ ad viam sive venellam, eundo et retornando ad portam ecclesiæ Sancti Petri, vocat Castell-strete;† in qua via sive venella murus anti-

* *Vicus Fullonum*—The street of the cloth workers. The whole manufacture of druggets, blankets, coarse cloth, and felts, was carried on in the three parishes which lie beyond the bridge over the Avon. "Fullo," "Towkere," and "Webbe," all signified a clothworker. The first clothier upon record is Thomas Blankett.—*Rot. Pat. 7 Edw. 3tij.*

† *Peter*-street, originally *Castle*-street, the modern *Castle*-street having been built upon the site and with the ruins of the Castle, 1654—1660.

quus portæ villæ Bristoll. scituabatur citra tenementa patris mei, (quondam Agnetæ Randolf,) in quibus unus aurifaber manet, modo, in anno Christi 1480, et de novo edificavit dicta duo tenementa in sinistra manu eundo ad portam novam Newgate: continet tota predicta via a porta Sancti Leonardi directè eundo per Corne-strete ac per altam crucem et per ecclesias Sanctæ Werburgæ et Sanctæ Trinitatis, ac directè eundo per Vinch-stret* ab antiquo vocatum Tour-strete, dimittendo murum antiquum villæ ac antiquissimam portam villæ citra Pyttey-yate aliter dict. Ayllewardes† yate in sinistra manu dicta antiquissima porta scita in vico de Pyttey super montem de Pyttey, prope vicum de Toure-strete, eundo ad portam antiquissimam vocatam . . . . prope cimiterium Sancti Johannis Baptistæ; et sic longitudo predictæ longæ viæ a porta Sancti Leonardi, directa linea eundo per officium domus justitiæ de le pyllorye usque ad illam venellam quæ ducit in eundo versus ecclesiam Sancti Petri, in loco principii dictæ viæ sive loco erat antiquis temporibus porta antiqua scita citra ‡*juniorem* portam de

---

‡ "new."

---

* *Vinch*-street, not *Wine*-street, which is a subsequent corruption. "Vicum vocatum Wine-street." 1457. I conjecture that Wynch, the first name given to this street, referred to the Pillory or Collistrigium, commonly called "the Wynch," which was erected near the east end of it, and was placed on a turning beam. "Wynch" means a tourniquet or windlass, as a "Wynch Well."

† Aylward's, or the "Old Gate," in distinction to "New Gate."

Newgate modo prostrata ac murum antiquissimum Bristolliæ, quæ predicta via sic incipiendo a porta Sancti Leonardi in occidente scita ad locum portæ antiquissimæ [u]*sic dirutæ* in parte orientali prope castrum villæ continet in longitudine 580 gressus.

Via vocata **Irysh*-meade aliter Rush-lane scita directe ad finem viæ de Brode-mede in parte boriali ecclesiæ fratrum predicatorum vocat. Castel-frerys, et via Mareshalle-strete veniente de castro intersecat viam Brode-mede et dictam viam de Irys-mede super quandam pontem lapideam in inceptione dictæ viæ; et longitudo ejus a principio viæ de Brode-mede usque ad quandam antiquam viam sive venellam scitam in orientali parte, et boriali, ultra ecclesiam fratrum predicatorum veniente ab antiquis temporibus per viam de Kyngys-strete de campis borialibus villæ Bristolliæ ex parte Horfelde et Rydyng-felde ad antiquum mercatum villæ Bristolliæ per orientalem partem chori dictorum fratrum vocat. Castell-frerys aliter frere-prechours, et in dicta via olim coci et venditores victualium ibi manebant diebus antiquis,† et longitudo dictæ viæ continet 370 gressus vel circa; latitudo predictæ viæ continet 14 gressus.

---

u " thus dilapidated."

---

* Qy. Rush? now Rosemary-lane.

† These were cooks and sellers of victuals, established there when the garrison of the Castle was constantly full, as it was in the reigns of K. John and Henry III. (1217)—" olim " " et temporibus antiquis."

De voltis, de archis et cellariis de petra factis cum mearenno et arbore coopertis secundum informationem Willelmi Clerk de vico Seynt Mary the Port-strete, die sabbato . . . septembris, anno Christi 1480.

In Hygh-strete sunt 19 wolta archuata et 12 cellaria, de voltis vero in toto 31.

In Bradstrete ultra 20 volta et cellaria.

In Corn-strete sunt 20 volta et cellaria.

In Pyttey aliter Aylewarde-street, in orientali parte viæ altæ ubi antiqua porta villæ est edificata prope vicum strictum de Toure-strete, eundo versus ecclesiam Sancti Johannis per Blynde-yate, sunt 4 cellaria.

In Wynch-strete sunt 27 volta et cellaria, 3 in. .

In vico Shamelys, volta quam lata longa et profunda 12, continet quælibet volta longitudinis 12 virgas.

In Seynt Marye Port-strete in utraque parte viæ sunt 15 volta et cellaria.

In Radclyff-strete sunt plura volta et cellaria.

In Shamely quondam Worshyp-strete sunt 12 volta et cellaria in una parte kyngys-shamelys.

In Seynt Colas strete sunt ultra 12 volta et cellaria.

In Smal strete sunt . . . volta et cellaria circa 12 et ultra.

In **Hoor*-strete aliter Horstrete sunt ultra 6 cellaria seu volta.

* William Hore or Hoor was Mayor in 1312, 5 Edw. II., and probably resided in this street. 12 Edw. 3tij. 1338, John Le Hoor covenants to build a stone wall of sixty feet

In vico Brode-mede una volta de petra constructa de propriis expensis Willelmi Botoner dict. W. Worcestre in anno Christi 1428.*

The Halle of the chapell† of Seynt Vincent of Gyston-clyff ys IX yerdes long.

And the brede ys 3 yerdys.

The length of the kechyn ys . . . . yerdes.

in length, in "Scapefulle strete," near the Town Marsh. His seal, an "eagle displayed," is affixed to this deed.

Le Hore.

Argent, an Eagle displayed within a bordure engrailed, sable.

Thomas Hore was Sheriff in 1449, 27 Henry VI.

* The number of the Vaults and Cellars in the principal streets was 169, besides those in the piers of the bridge and the other side of the river.

† At present we should search in vain for any ledge or station of the rock, upon which a hermitage of the size specified could have been placed. There are some expressions in Wyrcestre's account of it, which lead us to suppose that the cave called Foxhole, was capacious enough to have contained these apartments. The height as described above the river, and the steps of descent from the main land, authorise this opinion, as well as that it was not less than forty feet deep and proportionably wide and high. There was likewise a chapel dedicated to our Lady in the rock at Dover, which was visited by Henry VII.—*See Household Book.*

And the brede of the kechyn ys 3 yerdes.

And from the chapelle of Seynt Vyncent ys to the lower water 40 vethym.

And from the ovyr part of the mayn grounde londe of the seyd hygh rok downe to the seyd chapelle of Seynt Vyncent ben xx vethym rekened and proved; and so from the hygh mayne ferme londe of the seyd rok downe to the lowest water ground of the channel of Avyn and Frome is 60 vethym and much more, proved by a yong man of smythys occupacion yn Radclyff-strete, that seyd yt to me, hath both descended from the hyghest of the rok downe to the water syde.

Fons est ibidem circa lowshot apud le blak rok in parte de Ghyston-clyff in fundo aquæ, et est ita calidus sicut lac vel aqua Badonis.[v]

Scarlet-welle est fons preclarissimus emanens de alta rupe in parte opposita aquæ in dominio *de Lye*,[w] et est in altitudine in altiori parte de le rok de parte villæ de Lye altitudinis 12 pedum.

Rok Breke-faucet per unum jactum lapidis versus Bristolliam in parte Ghyston-clyff.

Fox-hole est volta mirabiliter scita super in alto de Ghyston-clyff super ripam de le rokk altiorem, et valde periculosus locus ad intrandam voltam, ne cadat in mari profunditatis 60 brachiorum et ultra.

De heremitagio et capella Sancti Vincentii in quadam rupe altissima sive scopula durissima et profunditatis usque ad[x] *aquam venientem de Bristollia, viz.*

Latitudo aulæ heremitagii est 7 virgæ.

---

[v] Bath. [w] Leigh. [x] "when the tide was out."

Longitudo capellæ Sancti Vincentii 8 virgæ.
Latitudo capellæ Sancti Vincentii 3 virgæ.
Longitudo domus coquinæ 6 virgæ.

Viæ ascensus de capella in rupe 20 brachiorum circa medium rupis Ghyston-clyff ascendendo ad terram altam, eundo et ascendendo per W. Botoner dict. Worcestre, eundo et numerando die dominica 26 die mensis Septembris, in anno Christi 1480, continet dicta altitudo a capella heremitagii 124 gressus; et sic patet, quod quilibet ascensus in eundo contra aliquem montem semper secundum racionem altitudinis 20 brachiorum, anglice a vathym, computabitur in altitudine ascensus 124 gressus vel circa.

*Viæ de Horstrete** de porta Frome-yate, eundo per ecclesiam Sancti Bartholomei, eundo per figuram Beatæ Mariæ virginis in muro horti carmelitarum, sic eundo usque ad bakkam Sancti Augustini, continet ad edificationem dictæ viæ in parte sinistra versus aquam de Frome 420 gressus.

Longitudo trium domorum magnificarum et magnæ altitudinis vocat *le Seynt Mary port*† cum profunda volta de lapidibus archuata in profundi-

* *Hore*-street was at first corrupted into *Horse*-street; now, by a pretended correction, it is written and called *Host*-street, because, it is said, that the Host was carried in procession through it. This was not done exclusively, for whenever the ceremony was required for any person "*in articulo mortis,*" it was taken to him through any street in the town.

† Called likewise in several old wills "Ecclesia B. M. Virginis in Foro." The market for the town was originally held there; and for the Castle in the Old Market—"veyl mercate." The ancient "Bocherew," now the site of Bridge-street, stood in this parish.

tate graduum quasi circa 40 gradus, id est steppys, continens in longitudine a vico de lez shambles usque intrando in domibus tribus magnis predictis 18 virgas.

Longitudo rupis Ghyston-clyff est inceptio per spacium duorum miliarium ab Hygh-strete cruce Bristolliæ, eundo per villulam Clyffton, cujus dominus villæ est N . . . Broke, dominus Cobham.*

Breke-faucet est quædam rupis in Ghyston-clyff, locus periculosus pro obviatione navium tempore introitus navium tam magnorum quam parvorum.

* John Broke, Baron Cobham, summoned to Parliament 1472, 12 Edw. IV. The manor of Clifton was afterwards granted to Sir John Chokke, Chief Justice.

Brooke.

Gules on a cheveron, argent, three lions, rampant, sable.

In the chancel of Redcliff church is the following monumental inscription :—

Hic jacet corpus venerabilis viri Johannis Brook quondam servientis ad legem illustrissimi principis felicis memoriae regis Henrici octavi et justiciarii ejusdem regis pro assisas in partibus occidentalibus Angliae et capitalis seneschali illius honorabilis domus et monasterii Beatae Mariae de Glasconia in comitatu Somerset, qui quidem Johannes obiit 25 die mensis Decembris Anno Domini millesimo quingentessimo 25°, et juxta eam requiescit Johanna uxor ejus una filiarum et heredum Richardi A merike, quorum animabus propitietur Deus, Amen.

quorumcunque ponderum seu quantitatis fuerunt, in fundo aquæ de Frome et Avyn venientium de Bristollia; et[y] *morabitur navis supra dictum Brekefaucet, quousque fluxus marinus fluendo ad portum Bristolliæ accrescet*, et distat a rupe et capella Sancti Vincentii versus Bristolliam per spacium jactus sagittæ.

Ledes sunt rupes fractæ profundissimæ in inferiore parte aquarum de Avyn et Frome currente de Bristollia, et dictæ rupes fractæ continent latitudinem totius aquæ de le chanelle a loco vocato le Ghyston-clyff transmeando ad aliam partem rupis alterius partis vocat. rupis in dominio villæ de Ashton *Lye*[z] de comitatu Somerset, directe in opposita parte Ghyston-clyff, ubi portus de Hungrode cum navibus magnis intrant.

Et dictæ rupes fractæ, quando non fluit mare, faciunt naves ex *carente aqua*[a] subitò descendere in infimum locum anglice dictum aldere-fall.

Via longa de Kyngystrete apud Beggher-welle continuata, quæ via venit de Monken brygge, incipiendo dictam viam de Kyngstrete ad Beggherwelle continet . . . gressus.

Et sic a dicta via de Beggher-welle continuando viam directa via in sinistra manu de Erlesmede usque ad finem occidentalem dicti prati, continet longitudo a dicta fonte vocata Beggher-welle 840 gressus.

Via alia longa borialis, incipiendo a fine orientali

---

y "And a ship borne towards the port of Bristol, would be foundered upon the rock of Brekefaucet, at the influx of the tide."

z Legh. a "for want of water."

de *Erlesmede,** et directe retornando ad pontem le bryg citra molendinum quondam diebus meis vocatum Bagpath-mylle, in quo loco ut aliqui dicunt libertas et franchesia villæ Bristolliæ extendit usque dictum pontém, qui est pars orientalissima et finis orientalis dicti [b]*pulchri prati*, per quam pontem aqua de Frome transit per dictum pontem, et sic continue transit per latus meridionale dicti *famosi* prati et per castrum villæ par latus vici de la Weer.

Et sic longitudo retornacionis dicti prati ad caput finis quadranguli per dictum pontem orientalem citra predictum molendinum, vocatum Bagpath-mille, continet in latitudine dictiErles-medew 300 gressus.

Ecclesia fratrum carmelitarum, viz., navis ecclesiæ, continet 45 gressus.

Latitudo ejus continet 25 gressus.

Latitudo turris campanilis continet 5 gressus.

Chorus ecclesiæ fratrum predicatorum continet 45 gressus.

Claustrum eorum ex omnibus 4 partibus continet 40 gressus.

Ecclesia religiorum vocat. le Gauntes, videlicet navis ecclesiæ, continet 43 gressus in longitudine.

Latitudo ejus continet 26 gressus.

Sanctuarium locum Sancti Augustini ab oriente ubi introitus sanctuarii est in occidentem ad por-

---

[b] "fair meadow."

---

* So called, as being part of the original demesne of the Castle, when founded by Robert Consul, Earl of Gloucester.

tam extremam [c] *ad intrandam curiam abbatis de officiis domorum, granariorum, pistorum, pandoxatorum, stablaorum, pro dominis,* &c. continet 360 gressus eundo juxta ecclesiam Sancti Augustini.

Latitudo dicti Sanctuarii a porta predicta ad venellam intrantem vocat. Froglane continet 240* gressus.

Latitudo sive distantia loci ab occidentali parte portæ de Gauntes ad portam introitus ecclesiæ abbathiæ Sancti Augustini continet ex transverso 180 gressus.

Frog-lane incipiendo ad borialem finem ecclesiæ de Gauntes† intrando per orta et gardinam de lez Gauntes et per murum *fratrum carmelitarum*‡ usque

---

" [c] entering into the Abbot's court of offices, granaries, bakehouse and brewhouse, and stables for his horses," or those of the superior guests,—*Dominorum.*

---

* Wyrcestre in various of his MSS., which I have examined, always uses the *half eight* ɐ for the 4, which has rendered several of his measurements obscure or incorrect, in the transcription.

† Annexed to the College of "Bonhommes" (commonly called the Gaunts, from the name of the original founders) were a large orchard and garden, upon which Orchard-street now stands. Upon the lower part of Stony-hill, adjoining, stood their columbarium, "Culver, or pidgeon house," upon which Culver-street is now built with houses, some of which are upon terraces, with gardens, "horti pensiles." There were only two other Colleges of Bonhommes in England, at Ashridge in Buckinghamshire, and at Edington in Wiltshire.

‡ Carmelite or White Friars.

ad Styp-strete altitudinem ubi fons est de frestone versus ecclesiam Sancti Michaelis continet 660 gressus.

Venella magna vocat le pryour ys lane Sancti Jacobi, quæ apud le style in angulo cornerii de Lewynesmede usque ad murum extremum directum super Montague-hill, eundo per murum *fratrum Sancti Francisci** ex una parte et murum monacorum ex orientali, continet usque returnum ad montem Sancti Michaelis directa linea 360 gressus, scilicet sic retornando venellam ad ecclesiam Sancti Michaelis per continuationem dictæ venellæ versus occidentem.

Venella a capite anguli muri *fratrum minorum*† vocat le pryour lane monachorum in parte occidentali, sic eundo ad montem Sancti Michaelis versus ejus ecclesiam usque ad locum et montem vocat Styp-strete prope fontem de frestone, continet . . gressus.

Vicus de Shamelys ab antiquo vocatus *Worshyp strete*,‡ ubi portus navium et lenarum existebat, continet in longitudine a porta Sancti Nicholai, directe eundo ad quandam finem loci viæ quadratæ, 300 gressus.

Vicus defensorius§ incipiente ad finem viæ vocatæ

* Franciscan Friars, Minorites, or Grey Friars.

† The Benedictine Monks of St. James, a cell to the Abbey of Tewkesbury.

‡ In Worship-street, were the King's Storehouses for his prisage of Wool and Wine, on the banks of the Avon, above the bridge.

§ The "Vicus defensorius" or Defence-lane, was built against a very strong and lofty wall by the Burgesses, after le Shamelys, directe incipiendo ad locum rectum quadrati per vicum de extransverso de Seynt Peter-strete coram novo fonte facto [c] *de bonis Canyngs** de alta domo de frestone ab exteriore parte via de Wynch-strete continet 135 gressus.

Via parva quamvis lata in occidentali parte ecclesiæ omnium sanctorum et collegii kalendarii prope ibidem intrando versus meridiem in parte juxta cimiterium dictæ ecclesiæ continet 60 gressus.

Collegium presbiterorum vocatum le kalenders in occidentali parte ecclesiæ omnium sanctorum, in quo collegio Thomas Botoner avunculus meus fuit frater collegii, et sepelitur in meridionali novæ elæ ecclesiæ omnium sanctorum, ab antiquo fundatum diu ante conquestum Willelmi Conquestoris.

Domus conducti aquæ pulchra sub domo kalendarii est scituata.

De capella Sanctæ Annæ per duo milliaria de Bristollia.†

Quidam dominus De le Warr fundavit primo capellam Sanctæ Annæ.

---

c "out of Canynge's Estate."

---

the memorable siege of the Castle, in the reign of Edward the Second.

* By virtue of the Will of W. Canynges, in 1474, his residuary property in Bristol was given to W. Spenser, his Executor, in trust to the Corporation, for public works, provided, his grandchildren, William and Agnes, died minors, which happened. Spenser built this fountain, near St. Peter's, and a hospital.

† The Chapel of St. Anne was situated in the parish of

Capella Sanctæ Annæ continet in longitudine 19 virgas.

Latitudo ejus continet 5 virgas.

Et sunt de boterasses circa capellam 19.

Item sunt duæ cereæ anglice quadratæ,* una de dono officii artis wevers, de terra ad cooperturam archuati volti continet altitudo 80 pedes.

Et densitudo unius ceræ quadratæ lez [e] *officium artis corduanarii* continet in latitudine 10 pollices fere unius pedis.

Et in densitate 8 pollices.

Et cera quadrata data per [f] *officium artis textorum*

---

[e] "Guild of Shoemakers." [f] "Guild of Weavers."

Brislington, near the banks of the Avon. It was held in high consideration, and was much frequented by the inhabitants of Bristol, by way of pilgrimage, on account of its supposed superior sanctity. Elizabeth of York, wife of K. Henry VII., when at Bristol in 1502, went to make an offering there.—*See her Privy Purse Accounts. Nicolas.* This Chapel of St. Anne was originally founded by one of the Barons La Warr, probably by the same who founded the Hospital of St. Bartholomew in Bristol. It was an insulated building, supported by 19 buttresses. Length 57 feet (interior) by 15, which are the dimensions of a considerable structure.

* Square wax lights for the Altar, given by guilds or companies of artificers, established in Bristol. Such wax lights were called "mortars." These contributions were annually renewed, and are still made by artisans in the Catholic countries.

anglice wefers continet in longitudine ad voltam capellæ 80 pedes

Latitudo 8 pollices.

Densitudo 7 pollices.

Et quolibet anno dictæ cereæ sunt renovatæ erga diem pentacost.

Et quælibet cera quadrata ex ponderibus ceræ et factura constabat 5 libr.

Et sic duæ predictæ cereæ constabant 10 libr.

Et sunt in dicta capella 32 *naves et naviculæ** ac de caracis navibus.

Et sunt de navibus de argento formatis et factis 5 naves, precium cujuslibet navis 20s.

Et coram ymagine Sanctæ Annæ sunt 13 cereæ quadratæ, appreciatæ ad . . .

In orientali via de Radclyf chyrch, capellæ Beatæ Mariæ, est murus longus versus Pyle-hille fontem, ad eundem ad Sanctam Annam; continet dictus murus in longitudine 50 virgas sive 70 gressus per [g]*filium meum* numeros virgarum numerat. ad incepcionem muri prope orientalem partem cimiterii dictæ ecclesiæ.

Et ab inceptione dicti [h]*muri* in orto *claudati*

---

g Lewis. h "stone-wall inclosure."

---

* Small vessels made of silver to receive and contain offerings, and sometimes to burn incense in. William of Wykeham bequeaths to the Cathedral of Winchester "one elemosynary dish in the form of a ship." Among Cardinal Wolsey's plate was "oone lytell shippe for francincense silvar and parcell-gilte—poiss. x oz." The quantity of plate belonging to parish Altars, Chapels, and Chantries, may be thus accounted for.

juxta cimiterium orientalis partis muri predicti a dicto merestone, in eadem parte eundo per cimiterium predictum juxta collegium capellanorum Willelmi Canyngys ad domum camerarum dictorum capellanorum continet in latudine 150 gressus.

Latitudo viæ de Radclyff-hill de cameris presbiterorum predictorum ad alteram partem domorum [i]*operariorum de frestone pro fundacione ecclesiæ* de Radclyff, sunt 40 gressus.

Et a loco camerarum Willelmi Canyngys in fine occidentali cimiterii predicti usque ad Radclyff yate continet circa 180 gressus.

Columna principalis quatuor columpnarum, quæ portant turrim competentem [k]*coram hostium chori* occidentalis ecclesiæ Radclyff continet 103 bowtells.*

Circumferentia principalium columpnarum, et quælibet earum quatuor columpnarum continet 6 virgas.

Circumferentia aliarum columpnarum tocius ecclesiæ continet 4 virgas.

Latitudo viæ de Radclyff-stret coram turrim ecclesiæ de Radclyff continet 14 gressus, et eadem latitudo durat infra Radclyff-strete.

Via infra Radclyff-strete per murum vocatum le toune-wall eundo versus Seynt Thomas strete, cujus sinistra pars viæ est bene edificata, et altera

---

[i] Freestone masons, the builders of Redcliffe Church. [k] "before the entrance into the Choir."

---

* Boltellæ. Bowtells—perpendicular mouldings surrounding the shaft of a pillar.

pars, dextra manu, est murus vocatus le toune walle, continet in longitudine 152 gressus.

Longitudo viæ de le toune walle ad Seynt Thomas strete de angulo ex parte . . . de muro edificatorum eundo ad pontem Bristol continet 660 gressus.

Latitudo de Brodemede* continet 28 gressus.

Latitudo brevis viæ de Kyngys-strete a principio dictæ viæ prope turrim de Monkyn-brygge in quadam venella usque le style ad eundum ad cimiterium Sancti Jacobi in parte [1]*anguli hospicii*† Willelmi Pownam apud crucem et pontem, eundo

---

1 "corner of the dwelling-house."

---

* The "Broade mede" in the parish of St. James, was the first inhabited part of it, as appendant to the town, and as such, was granted to the priory by William Earl of Gloucester, by patent. t. Hen. 2di. Patent of Inspeximus 2do. Hen. 4ti. m. 7. "totum novum burgum de Prato apud Bristolliam"—meaning that it was *then* first covered with buildings.

† An ancient tenement or house, during the early centuries, as inhabited by the Burgesses of Bristow, was thus constructed. The souterrain was a very large cellar (cellarium) with a groined and ribbed roof of stone, and when extending under the street, divided by arches and pillars. Such instances are not so frequent as those covered by timber beams. In these were deposited the heavier goods. The ground floor was divided into narrow shops (shopæ) three or four upon the same ground plan, with stalls or bulk heads, and open to the street. They were for daily traffic with the inhabitants, and numerous frequenters of the town. In the houses of the chief merchants there was built behind these shops, a hall (aula),

in dicta via per lez barrys et usque Erlesmede continet 100 gressus; et a principio cimiterii Sancti Jacobi eundo per lez barrys, eundo ad pratum Erlysmede.

Latitudo viæ in principio de Lewenysmede prope ecclesiam Sancti Jacobi 8 gressus eundo usque Frome-yate.

Crux decens de frestone erecta super arcum voltæ unius gradus viæ intrantis ad aquam de Frome, anglice a slypp, in vico Knyfesmyth-strete, aliter Cristmas strete.

Venella brevis scita in angulo ultra crucem predictam ad quendam hostium usque aquam de Frome per prope Frome-yate in boriali parte predictæ crucis continet in longitudine circa 60 gressus in fine Cristmasse strete.

Crucis latitudo de Hygh-strete, continet 2 virgas.

De Cellariis etc.

In alto vico, Hygh-strete, sunt in parte orientali of the hygh-crosse de Seynt Cholas yate 17 cellarii.

Et in opposita parte occidentali dicti Hygh-strete sunt 12 cellarii.

Item in Corn-strete, de cruce alta, in parte boriali vici ad portum Sancti Leonardi per ecclesiam Sanctæ Werburgæ sunt 18 cellarii computati.

with a high arched roof of timber frame. It served commonly to hold linen, woollen, and spices, and the more valuable goods, and at set times for their feasts. The first floor contained the habitable house (Cameræ) bedrooms, parlour (parlatorium), kitchen (coquina), all of which are mentioned in deeds and wills. And lastly (Solaria) garrets, which had two projecting stories under the roof.

Item in parte meridionali viæ de alta cruce eundo per ecclesiam omnium sanctorum sunt 17 cellarii.

Venella parvissima de Hyghstrete juxta meridionalem partem ecclesiæ omnium sanctorum et officium cocorum contiuet 60 gressus.

Item in vico Bradstrete eundo ab alta cruce ad partem orientalem de Bradstrete per ecclesiam Sanctæ Trinitatis continet 15 cellaria.

Item eundo in parte occidentali dictæ viæ per tenementum magistri Willelmi Botoner ac domum Gyldhalle ac capellam Sancti Georgii, sunt 15 cellaria.

In Wynch-strete, aliter Castel-strete, ab alta cruce in parte dextra sive meridionali dictæ viæ per le pyllory eundo ad portam New-gate sunt 21 cellarii.

Et a dicta cruce eundo in Wynch-strete per latus boriale dictæ viæ continue usque ad portam Newgate 14 sunt cellarii, et alterius continuando ad finem orientalis viæ de le Weere per molendinum castri, sunt 10 cellaria.*

Domus justiciæ et officii collistrigii† scita circa medium de Wynch-strete coram finem viæ de Pittey-yate est rotundum, constructum de opere frestone decenter, tam amplitudinis quam altitudinis, cum cameris ac fenestris cum barris de ferro artificiose compactis, continet in spacio circuitus

* There were cellars or vaults, in all, 139, as above.

† It was a high frame of timber beams, and the punishment was very severe. Mr. Douce, in his illustrations of Shakspeare, has given a very curious account of "Collistrigia," from illuminations in ancient MSS.

domus dicti officii . . gressus. Et de [m]*super domus collistrigii* est instrumentum de arboribus opere carpentarii constructum ad [n]*collistrendum infames homines deliquentes in pistura, quarum tortarum etcæt.*

In Pyttey-strete infra Aylward-yate five Pytteyyate prope ibidem in magno spacio, veluti locus trianguli est fons ampla et profunda cum frestone bene circumdata et alta pro hominibus hauriendo aquam fontanam, et dicta fons [o]*bene tegulata desuper* ad custodiendum homines aquam haurientes de pluvia seu procellis; et sunt in boriali parte viæ Pittey 2 cellaria.

Officium domus latrinæ anglice a privey tam pro mulieribus quam hominibus in latitudine meridionali spacii dicti trianguli.

Longitudo viæ ab angulo principii pontis ad portam Sancti Nicholai sunt 9 virgæ.

Longitudo portæ Sancti Johannis Baptistæ 8 virgæ.

In vico Sancti Nicholai sunt 12 cellarii de porta Sancti Nicholai usque portam Sancti Leonardi.

In venella Sancti Leonardi prope cimiterium eundo in Smalstrete sunt plures voltæ sive cellarii de sub terra, quia [p]*tota venella est, et cimiterium est magnæ altitudinis respectu viæ trianguli de le kay* quasi circa 10 pedum subtus via cimiterii eundo ad Small-strete.

[m] "The house upon the platform of which the pillory was placed." [n] "Collistrigia—Neckstretchers for infamous men, delinquents in baking of bread, of which wrongs, &c." [o] "with a tiled penthouse above." [p] "The whole lane and churchyard are of great height, with respect to the triangular space upon the Quay."

In parochio Sancti Stephani.

Vicus Pylle-strete est via a Seynt Leonard ys yate ad triangulum venellarum ad orientalem fenestram altaris ecclesiæ Sancti Stephani, viz. venella una retro orientalem fenestram Sancti Stephani, [q] *venella alia apud le style ecclesiæ Sancti Stephani ad keyam dimittendo cimiterium in manu dextra*, et tercius vicus est longus incipiente a fine predicti Pylle-strete, et eundo per Merstrete longa via ad Merse yate.

Apud le kay in spacio trianguli largi est in medio dicti trianguli pulcherrima domus de frestone erecta [r] *sumptuose operata*, in qua est conductus aquarum de plumbo conduct. de fonte,* cujus principium fontis est apud . .

Via alia de Pyll-stret extendendo ad domum custumæ regis, ubi vendunt salsas pisces ad principium trianguli 64 gressus.

Cristmas-strete vel Knyf-smyth-strete continet in latitudine 12 gressus, id est . . virgas.

---

q "Another lane at the stile of St. Stephen's churchyard, leaving it on the right hand." r "of rich architecture."

---

* A castellet was a stone inclosure to contain the reservoir of water brought by pipes from a distant head, for the supply of the particular district. It was generally composed of ornamental architecture, and the top crenellated or embattled, whence that name. Leland particularises the several castellets in Bristol in his time. The last of them rebuilt in the reign of Elizabeth, attached to St. John's Church, was entirely removed in 1828. The castellet on the key, "a most beautiful house and sumptuously wrought in masonry," must have been the most remarkable, then, to

Viæ latitudo ad le key de Seynt Johnys yate continet 6 gressus.

Triangulus, qui est magnum et amplum spacium apud le key, ubi domus conducti aquæ in medio trianguli scituatur continet ex tribus partibus de le custom-hous ad keyam et de keya ad . .

Porta de Frome-yate, duæ portæ cum cathena ferri, cum vacuo spacio longitudinis dictarum portarum, continet 22 virgas super archus et duas portas edificatas.

Cristmastrete.

Pons sive archus sub una cruce decenti de frestone desuper erecta ad quendam angulum ad modum trianguli super pontem archus erecta in fine viæ vocatæ Cristmas-strete aliter knyfe-smyth-strete prope Frome-yate continet . . gressus.

Gradus, anglice [s]*a stepe,* subtus archus et crucem ad eundum ad aquam de Frome pro lotura vestimentorum lineorum seu laneorum in fine de Cristmastrete continet circa . . gressus.

Latitudo viæ de Cristmastrete incipiendo apud portam Sancti Johannis continet 12 gressus.

---

[s] "a slip."

---

be seen. It was probably built by one of the Frampton's, who had a large mansion near it, in 1480.

Castellets in Bristow. Cis pontem. St John's, hard by St. John's gate.

The Key Pipe, with a very fair castellet. (near St. Stephen's.)

St. Nicholas Pipe, with a castellet.

Ultra pontem. Redclive Pipe, with a castlet, harde by Redclive Churche. *Leland.* v. 7. f. 71.

Radcliff-hylle ultra ecclesiam.

Via de Radclyff-strete, incipiente in parte meridionali villæ Bristoll. ultra ecclesiam Radclyff apud angulum viæ ducentis ad Trillye-myllys* usque ad ultimam portam prope conductum portæ de Radclyff, continet novies 60 gressus, quod est 540 gressus.

Latitudo viæ majoris loci continet ex opposito turris campanilis Radclyff 12 gressus.

Memorandum quod longitudo turris campanilis in volta nova facta continet 24 pedes ab oriente in occidentem, et 22 pedes a boria in meridiem.

ᵗ *Item basis quadrati fabricationis speræ de Radclyff, quæ est de octo panis, primus cursus super locum quadraturæ speræ constat in densitudine lapidibus duorum pedum ex duabus petris cementatis, quia durum contrahere unum lapidem talis densitudinis, et sic continuat minuendo usque ad certam altitudinem, ac quatuor sconci de lapidibus ab uno quarterio anguli in proximum ad ligandam speram,* quæ quidem spera stat modo ultra 100 pedes.†

ᵗ "The base of the square building of the spire of Radclyff which consists of eight panes or pannels. The first course above the square part of the spire has the thickness of blocks of two feet, made by two stones cemented together, because it is difficult to contract or narrow a single stone of such thickness—and thus it continues to diminish to a certain height; and the four pinnacles of stone issue from each angle which tye or bind the spire." This is a curious architectural notice.

---

* Trene mills. Fulling mills made of wood in distinction to the stone molendina, for grinding corn.

† Are we to conclude that the Spire, after having been struck with lightning, was still 100 feet high? Does modo

Item domus longitudo presbiterorum Canyngis in longitudine 20 virgarum vel 19 virgarum, cum 4 baywyndowes de frestone pro cameris 4 presbiterorum.

Dedicacio ecclesiæ Sancti Johannis Baptistæ Bristoll. die 17 jullii.

Longitudo ecclesiæ Sancti Johannis Baptistæ 21 virgæ.

Latitudo ejus 8 virgæ.

Via vocata Radclyff-strete incipiendo a porta de Radclyff, continuando viam usque principium pontis Bristoll. continet 710 gressus.

Latitudo viæ continet 12 gressus.

Spacium tenementorum mansionum ex quolibet latere pontis* Bristoll 10 virgas continet.

Item spacium interceptum in loco latrinarum

apply to W. W.'s time? It has not such an elevation now. "Stat modo" is certainly the present time. Perhaps it was written "stetit modo," stood once, or not long since.

* Comparison of the ancient bridges of London and Bristol. London bridge begun in 1176, completed in 1205, by Isenbert de Xainctes, a Norman architect, who built the bridge there. It was 926 feet long and 40 wide, having 19 broad pointed arches, and was covered with houses. The chapel of St. Thomas a Becket was erected upon the tenth pier; was 40 feet high, and had a plain gable only surmounted by a cross, with four buttresses, with crocketed finials, dividing the western end into three parts. In the interior were two stories, both consecrated to sacred purposes, and the roof of the lower was richly vaulted. The street of houses was complete on either side, which were of timber frame, and chiefly of large dimensions. One was so remarkable as to have been called the "Nonsuch." There were likewise two large towers with gateways.

officii* super pontem ad inceptionem mansionum primæ partis pontis de Radclyff-strete veræ incepcionis pontis continet 18 virgas.

Le Bakk Bristolliæ.

Via vocata le bak, ubi naves Walliæ intrant, continet a principio domus conductæ prope pontem usque ad portam extremam vocatam Mersh-yate in longitudine 3030 gressus per aquam Avon.

Latitudo dictæ viæ vocatæ le bak ad projiciendum bosca et alias mercandizas continet secundum majus et majus 30 gressus.

Altitudo maris Avone, quando novus refluxus maris est, [u]*in prima die commutacionis lunæ, ut*

[u] "In the first day of the change of the moon, as I have seen and heard, in the first lunation after the entrance of the sun into libra, the rise of the spring tide at the Bak is 7 or 8 fathom, at least 40 feet."

Both the chapel and Nonsuch house were occupied as warehouses for stationery goods, since the reformation, and which remained till 1758, when the whole was taken down, and the platform and arches of the bridge were reconstructed.

Of Bristol Bridge there was a general coincidence, excepting that it was so much smaller. It was built between the years 1240 and 1247. The breadth of the river is 200 feet. The bridge was built upon four arches, between very large and wide piers and starlings. The street was continued on either side, having some spacious houses, the road between them being no more than 19 feet. Of the chapel dedicated to the Assumption of the Virgin Mary, built by Elyas Spelley, Mayor in the reign of Edw. III. W. W. afterwards gives a particular account. The bridge was rebuilt between 1761 and 1768; when the houses which remained after the conflagration in 1644 were taken down.

* Mentioned in Canning's Will as Avon's Privey. There was another in the Pithay.

vidi et audivi in lunacione proxima ante introitum solis in libram est 7 vel 8 brachia apud le bak, anglice vathym, et brachium continet 6 pedes.

Viæ longitudo vocatæ Baft-strete incipiente ex opposito crucis in Baldwyne-strete usque murum villæ in opposito de le Mersh, continet [w]*a retro capellæ de le bak* in occidentali parte dictæ capellæ 240 gressus.

Latitudo dictæ viæ ad spacium 180 gressuum continet 20 gressus, sed in prima incepcione viæ apud crucem in Baldwyne-strete per spacium longitudinis 60 gressuum ejus latitudo est stricta via nisi latitudinis 3 virgarum.

Viæ quatuor ex omni latere in occidentali parte capellæ de le bak in edificatione quadrata per A. B. facta continet ex quolibet 4 lateribus . . gressus.

Porta Sancti Nicholai continet a boria in meridiem in longitudine 7 virgas.

Latitudo viæ de Hygh-strete finiente ad dictam portam continet 20 gressus.

Porta Sancti Leonardi continet ex parte orientali in longitudine 7 virgas.

Altitudo portæ cum campanile continet per estimacionem . . .

Latitudo viæ vocatæ Smalstrete ad finem portæ Sancti Leonardi continet 30 gressus.

Porta Sancti Johannis Baptistæ continet in longitudine a boria in meridiem versus Bradstrete 7 virgas, et ab oriente in occidentem versus le kay latitudo viæ de Bradstrete ad finem dictæ portæ continet 28 gressus.

[w] "behind the chapel on the Back."

Latitudo viæ vocatæ Seynt Laurens lane continet 6 gressus.

Portæ duæ super pontem de Frome-yate continet in longitudine . . virgas vel 34 gressus.

Pons duorum archuum aquam de Frome transeuntium continet in longitudine . . virgas . . gressus.

Obiit Johannes Barstable burgensis villæ Bristoll. A.D. 1411, quinto decimo kalend. Octobris, et habuit Nicholaum Barstable presbiterum magistrum capellæ Sanctæ Trinitatis.

Ecclesia Sanctæ Werburgæ* continet in latitudine 19 virgas vel 34 gressus.

* Darby.

Argent a cheveron engrailed between 3 garbs sable.

Deseent of Darby from Wills.

Walter Darby, of the parish of St. Werburg. Will dated 1385. Mayor 1367. = Joan

Walter Darby, Founder of St. Werburgh's Church. = Christina

William | Joan | John | Alice ux. W. Warminster, | Isabel ux. John Barstaple.

Turris quadratus dictæ ecclesiæ continet ex omni parte [x]*quatuor costarum* 5 virgas.

Tour-strete : longitudo viæ de Wynch-strete apud le pyllorye continuans per cimiterium Sancti Johannis prope blynde-yate usque Brad-strete continet 370 gressus.

Latitudo dictæ viæ continet ad minus 2 virgas, sed a orientali parte ecclesiæ Sancti Johannis Baptistæ continet 3 virgas.

Porta vocata Blynd-yate continet in latitudine 9 pedes, et in latitudine viæ 3 virgas id est 9 pedes desuper edificata.

Longitudo ecclesiæ Sanctæ Werburgæ continet 21 virgas.

Latitudo ejus 19 virgæ.

Turris ecclesiæ quadratæ continet 5 virgas ex omni latere.

Columpnæ archus 6, fenestræ 6 in una parte, et in qualibet fenestra 5 panell, et totidem columpnæ et archus in alia parte.

Fenestra una in orientali et alia in occidentali . .

Venella viæ a vico de Smalstrete per ecclesiam Sanctæ Werburgæ ad introitum viæ vocatæ Seynt Colastrete continet 145 gressus, ex opposito venellæ viæ per spacium 32 graduum ad Baldwyne-strete.

Venella viæ ad Baldwyne-strete ex opposito superscriptæ, eundo per certos gradus inferiores ad numerum 32, et . . gressuum ad vicum Baldwyne-strete ex opposito crucis lapideæ continet cum dictis 32 gradibus gressuum et . . gressibus.

[x] "four sides."

Via ab ecclesia Sancti Nicholai cum 5 gressibus areæ dictæ ecclesiæ ad introitum ecclesiæ voltæ vocatæ le [y]*crowd*, cum spacio latitudinis voltæ de dicta ecclesia arcus ac spacio latitudine 20 gressibus ad descensum voltæ de le croude ultra dict. 20 gressus præter 2 virgas.

Tamen longitudo tocius voltæ cum duobus alis ex numero 5 [z]*pyllerys archuatis* continet 12 virgas.

Et 5 magnæ columpnæ ac 5 archus sunt in dicta cripta five volta.

Item turris quadratus campanilis ecclesiæ predictæ continet 5 virgas ex omni parte.

Ad ecclesiam Sancti Michaelis.

Via in occidentali parte ecclesiæ Sancti Bartholomei Bristolliæ eundo ad ecclesiam Sancti Michaelis super altissimum montem, a via vocata le Stype-strete, incipiendo a collegio Sancti Bartholomei semper ascendendo ad quandam fontem et crucem lapideam in monte Sancti Michaelis, sic eundo ad *ecclesiam religiosarum Beatæ Mariæ Magdalenæ, pauperis religionis trium monacharum continet 360 gressus.

Et a dicta ecclesia religiosa sive ecclesia parochiali Sancti Michaelis usque ad lapidem altum

---

y Crypt. z "Pillars which support arches."

---

* This was the nunnery of St. Mary Magdalene, consisting only of three professed nuns, but of many novices, by whom the daughters of the principal inhabitants were educated. At the reformation they were held in so great estimation, that the visitors strongly recommended that they should not be dissolved, but without effect.

assignatum pro limite franchesiæ villæ Bristolliæ, prope crucem et locum furcarum pro justitia legis pro traditoribus et latronibus suspendendis et executione mortis, 420 gressus ascendendo semper ad montem. Sed a dicta petra quæ est [a]*finis franchesiæ Bristolliæ plagæ meridionalis ab alta cruce* ad locum justiciæ exequend continet in toto, cum 120 gressis, 540 gressus.

Capella sanctæ crucis super Thyrdam-doune versus collegium de Westberye continet in longitudine 9 virgas.

Latitudo ejus continet 5 virgas et habet mantellum . . . .

Ecclesia collegii [b]*diaconata* de Westbery continet in longitudine 42 virgas vel LX gressus.

Latitudo ejus continet 24 virgas.

1447. Memorandum quod [c]*navis* Roberti Sturmey in primo viagio suo de Jerusalem fuit submersus prope Modon insulam* ex fortuna casu in nocte fracturæ, et 37 homines Bristolliæ suæ navis vocatæ le *Cog*† Anne, et ipsi 37 homines sepulti apud

---

[a] "The end of the Bristol liberties from the High Cross towards the South" [b] "having a Dean." [c] "ship belonging to."

---

* Modon is not an island, but a port on the continent of the Morea, not many leagues below the island of Zante, open to the Mediterranean. This vessel was conveying pilgrims or votarists to the Holy Sepulchre, a circumstance which caused the Bishop of Modon to consecrate an oratory to their memory. Robert Sturmye was one of the Merchants venturers. He was Sheriff in 1442, and Mayor in 1452.

† A Cog was a ship used to convey merchandize, but of the exact measure of its tonnage, we have no account.

Modon, et episcopus patriæ fecit capellam novam ad orandum pro animabus eorum.

*Touker-strete.**

Venella prima in Touker-strete de ponte Bristoll. continet 90 gressus ad aquam Avonæ.

Venella secunda versus Stallage-cros continet 100 gressus ad aquam de Avyn, et ista venella est apud Stallage-cros ex opposito.

Latitudo dictæ venellæ est 4 gressus.

* The first establishment and residence of the family of Canynge was in Tucker-street, which was entirely inhabited by clothiers or drugget makers, one of the more ancient manufactures in Bristol. W. Canynges made his will in 1396, and was buried in the chapel of Our Lady, in the church of St. Thomas, martyr. John, his son, in 1405, bequeaths his body to be buried in the same. "Item Johannæ ux. meæ 4 shopas situat' in Touker-strete, et duas aulas cum pertinentiis in vico predicto—unam aulam cum unâ shopâ adjacente in Touker-strete, &c., usque ad Lawditch posterius." The celebrated W. Canynge was their third son. By his will, dated 1474, he gives "duo tenementa unum in suburbiis villæ Bristol. in vico vocato West Touker-strete in parochiâ Sti. Thomæ Martyris inter tenementa Prioris Domûs Carthusianæ de Wytham, ex utrâque parte, et duo messuagia cum suis pertinentiis situat' super pontem Abonæ," &c. This property remained in the Canynge's family until its extinction by the death of the grand-children of W. Canynge, William and Isabel, during their minority, and not long after his own demise. John, their elder brother, is not mentioned in W. Canynge's will, because he inherited his mother's very ample jointure.

The manufacture of cloth was brought from Normandy to Bristol, and the West of England, early in the reign of Edward I. Clothworkers were called Toukers, from the river Toque, near Abbeville. In deeds of that date, these

Via in fine Toker-strete incipiendo a retro de Temple-strete ultra magnum fontem prope magnum et profundum gradum, anglice a stepe, in fine de Toker-strete, et eundo coram aquam de Avyn per prata in boriali parte aquæ continet ad retornam venellæ in Temple-strete ad le pyllorye 420 gressus; et dicta via est edificata in una parte versus dexteram manum, et alia pars viæ est cursus aquæ de Avyn.

Latitudo dictæ viæ est ultra circa 8 gressus, et aliquando 20 gressus.

Venella secunda existens coram aquam Avyn in dicta via versus ad Temple-strete continet 90 gressus.

Venella [d]*secunda in dicta via coram aquam de Avyn continet circa* 90 *gressus, et transit in retorno de quadam pervicina ponte arboris quod equus non transiet ad prata coram aquam Avyn*, et sic retornando ad Temple-strete ex opposito le pyllory prope ecclesiam Templi, continet ut super 90 gradus.

Latitudo dictæ venellæ continet 4 virgas.

---

d " a second lane in the same direction on the banks of the river Avon extends about 90 paces, and then turns off to a neighbouring bridge of wood, not passable by a horse, leading to meadows on the banks of the Avon."

---

several terms occur—Textor, Weaver; Fullo, Clothworker; Tinctor, Dyer; Feltere, Felt-maker; John le Tannere; Webbe; Chaucer calls his clothier, in the Canterbury Tales, "a Webbe." In 1334, a complaint was made against Thomas Blankett for having in his house foreigners, and foreign instruments of manufacture.

Ecclesia templi sanctæ crucis.

Longitudo ecclesiæ de templo sanctæ crucis continet 57 virgas, et circa 100 gradus per estimacionem.

Latitudo ejus continet 42 gradus.

Turris novus* ecclesiæ campanilis continet 5 virgas ex omni parte quadratæ.

Via subtus le toune-wallys incipiendo a parte Temple-strete, et eundo infra murum, juxta murum intrando per viam vocatam Seynt Thomas strete continet . . . gressus.

Venella in Temple-strete ultra ecclesiam templi ex parte meridionali de Temple-strete, id est in parte opposita ecclesiæ versus portam templi, quæ est secunda venella a cruce de Stallage-cross versus et ad Radclyffe-strete eundo . . . gressus.

Longitudo muri villæ Bristoll. transeundo per ortos Temple-yate, sed incipiendo ultra orientalem partem† cancellæ fratrum August. [e]*super borduram aquæ de Avyn*, continuando usque Temple-yate continet 600 gressus. Et sic continuando a porta

---

[e] "Upon the bank of Avon-water."

---

* It is most singular that William Wyrcestre does not mention the very extraordinary fact of the great declination of the original tower, adverting only to the addition made to it in his time. Indeed his *own* architectural notices are totally deficient; as he contented himself with mensuration only: but will the Itinerary of Leland always give satisfactory information, either by critical observation or comparison?

† This fixes the site of the small convent of the Hermits of the rule of St. Augustine, near to the Temple gate, but bordering on the banks of the river Avon. Founded in 1310 by Sir Simon, or Sir William, Montacute; to which

Temple-yate per muros villæ* ad primam portam de Radclyff-strete, qui est finis dictæ viæ de Radclyff-strete, continet 435 gressus.

Et sic in toto ab aqua Avonæ predictus murus continet usque ad portam primam de Radclyff-yate 1035 gressus.

Muri densitudo super viam quam homines ambulant 2 virgæ.†

Spissitudo tocius muri continet 2 virgas et duas pedes.

Venella in Radclyff-strete a prima porta Radclyff, vocata Hounden-lane, continet a via Radclyff usque Seynt Thomas strete in longitudine 170 gressus.

Latitudo dictæ venellæ continet 2 virgas.

Venella ex parte meridionali ecclesiæ Sancti Thomæ eundo juxta ecclesiam continet in longitudine 170 gressus.

last mentioned, a patent "de manso elargando" was granted in 1317. Sold in 1543 to Maurice Dennis.

* This is now the only remaining part of the town wall, and is partly perfect for several hundred yards to Redcliff-street; where the gate originally stood. It was built, or rather rebuilt, at the expense of the Butchers' Company. It now forms the boundary of gardens. In one of the earliest deeds now extant, dated in the year 1220, relating to tenements in Redcliff-street, the purchaser is T. Kull-bullock. In another a butcher is styled "Carnifex," a flesh-monger. "*Port Waulle* is the fairest part of the Towne waul. The sayinge is, that certein bochers made a fair peace of this waulle; and it is the highest and strongest peace of all the towne waulls."—*Leland* v. 7, f. 71.

† The space of six feet was sufficient for a publick walk or passage, or to man the walls during a siege. Such still remain at Chester and York.

Venella in parte boriali ecclesiæ Sancti Thomæ transeundo per cimiterium continet . . . . . .

Ecclesia Sancti Thomæ cum choro continet in longitudine 80 gressus.

Latitudo ejus continet 35 gressus.

Muri longitudo ex parte orientali villæ prope Pyttey-yate, incipiente in meridionali de Pyttey-yate, usque ad viam ducentem ad portam vocatam le Blynde-yate continet 170 gressus versus Monk-enbrygge, et continuando usque Frome-yate sic continet ulterius . . . . .

Muri villæ Bristoll. videlicet a principio de Frome-yate, et sic retornando usque per Lewlyns-mede, et retornando per Seynt Jamys bak et Brode-mede ac le [f]*bak parvum* usque Pyttey-yate, continet dictus murus per aquam de Frome gyrando 1000 gressus.

Via de fine Seynt Thomas-strete incipiente apud le toune-walle continuando sub le toune-walle ad portam primam de Radclyff-yate, qui est finis longæ viæ de Radclyff-strete, continet 170 gressus, edificata in parte orientali de le toune-walle.

Latitudo dictæ viæ continet 8 gressus.

Via incipiente apud occidentalem finem de cimiterio Radclyff-chyrch, sic transeundo per viam ducentem ad Trene-myllys, et continuando usque domum hospitalis Beatæ Mariæ Magdalenæ* in

---

[f] "the little Bec."

---

* The Matrix of the Seal of the Hospital of St. Mary Magdalene of Brightbow is still extant. It was founded for the reception of paupers afflicted with leprosy.

dextra manu, eundo versus pontem de Bryghtbow ad crucem et capellam dicti hospitalis, continet 300 gressus; et a dicta domo hospitalis usque pontem de Bryghtbow continet 230 gressus, ubi libertas villæ Bristoll. extendit, sic in toto 530 gressus.

Pons aquæ de Bryghtbow* versus ecclesiam hospitalis Sanctæ Katerinæ continet 24 gressus in longitudine.

Via predicta continuando a ponte de Bryghtbow versus Bedmynster ad capellam liberam hospitalis Sanctæ Katerinæ continet 170 gressus.

Via de hospitali ecclesiæ Sanctæ Katerinæ usque pontem vocat. Bryghtbow, eundo versus ecclesiam de Radclyff continet in longitudine 240 gressus.

Pons vocat Bryghtbow, ubi extrema pars libertatis villæ Bristoll. existens versus occidentem, eundo usque Wellys per Bedmynster continet 17 virgas longitudinis, sive 36 gressus.

Latitudo dicti pontis continet 5 virgas.

Viæ longitudo de porta vocata Radclyff-yate versus Bedmyster, et transeundo per ecclesiam Radclyff et domum mansionis presbiterorum Canyngys† usque ad pontem vocatum Bryghtbow, ubi ad dictum pontem libertas et franchesia villæ Bristolliæ extendit in occidentali parte villæ Bristoll. continet 1200 gressus.

* Bow is always applied to the single arch of a bridge; as at Stratford-le-Bow, near London, which Chaucer calls "Stratford-*at-the-Bow*."

† There were originally two Chantry priests in the church of St. Mary Redcliff, to which W. Canynges added three, and made them collegiate. He built a mansion for their residence in the churchyard, like those then newly-erected at Wells, by Bishop Beckington, for the Vicars-choral.

Portarum duarum predictarum in fine Radclyff-strete continet spacium longitudinis inter dictas duas portas 36 gressus.

Capella Sanctæ Mariæ Magdalenæ ab antiquo fundata cum hospitali gentium leprosarum scita est in parte boriali versus pontem de Bryghtbow ultra domum capellanorum Willelmi Canyngys, quæ capella scita est ultra viam ducentem ad molendinum vocatum Tremyllys, in altera parte cimiterii de Bedmynster.

De vico fratrum predicatorum vocato Marchall-strete.

Memorandum quod vicus vocatus Iryshmede in orientali parte de Marshall-strete continet in longitudine prope pontem lapidis juxta murum fratrum predicatorum . . . gressus.

Via vocata le Marchall-strete incipit ab angulo principii viæ De le Weer, eundo directe per fratres predicatores ad le barres, per tenementa patris mei W. Worcestre, et eundo continue per horrea prioratus Sancti Jacobi ad quandam metam de exteriori lapide libertatis villæ Bristoll. eundo ex parte boriali ad Rydyng-feld* et Westbury versus Glouces-triam, continet 1020 gressus.

* The field where Jousts and Tournaments were held. A military establishment, consisting of armed men, and always at the requisition of the King, was supported at the expense of the commonalty at large. After the removal of the garrison, they exercised and trained upon Kingsdown. It is evident from Wills, that the chief merchants were furnished with armour for their own use. In 1454, John Burton bequeaths to his brother Nicholas, two suits of plated armour, sufficient for two men; and Henry Gildeney, in 1430, two suits of armour, with a pole-axe and a lance, cuirasses and war-shoes, for each. Many more instances might be cited. Previously shirts of mail, with

Ecclesia fratrum predicatorum in Marshall-strete.

Via predicta vocata Marshall-strete, incipiendo directa linea de muro principii viæ vocatæ le Were prope angulum domus Bagpath, ex opposito duorum molendinorum villæ prope castrum villæ, et eundo per fratres predicatores, et transeundo per lez barres directe [g]*per horrea prioris Sancti Jacobi*, eundo per Redelond usque collegium Westbury, et per villamTokynton versus Aust-clyff ad Severn-water et Gloucestriam, continet 1020 gressus, unâ vice probatus per meos gressus; et dicta via de Marchall-strete habet finem ultra horrea prioratûs Sancti Jacobi ad quendam freestone longitudinis unius virgæ stantem.

Longitudo portarum vocat. Newyate continet 20 gressus.

Longitudo ecclesiæ Sancti Petri continet 54 gressus.

Longitudo edificacionis a retro ecclesiæ predictæ a via Sancti Petri ex orientali parte retornando versus aquam de Avyn continet 72 gressus, et consimili modo in retorno per dictum cimiterium ab orientali ecclesiæ Sancti Petri ad occidentalem partem dictæ ecclesiæ de edificatione [h]*magnifici hospicii* et tenementorum . . . Nortons continet 75 gressus.

Longitudo de Wynch-strete ex opposito Pyllery, eundo per caput viæ de Pyttey directe ad portam

---

[g] "through St. James's Barton." [h] "The spacious and handsome house."

---

hoods and gorgets, were in use, during the reign of Edward 3rd, when Bristol supplied to his great army, which invaded France, 222 soldiers. *M.SS. Smythe.*

Sancti Johannis, per cimiterium Sancti Johannis Baptistæ, continet 410 gressus ad portam Sancti Johannis Baptistæ transeundo.

Latitudo dictæ venellæ et viæ continet duas virgas, id est 6 pedes.

Ecclesia Sancti Mariæ de Port, continet cum campanile ejus longitudo 60 gressus.

Porta Sancti Johannis Baptistæ, super quam edificatur tam turris quadratus quam una spera de super de frestone cum duobus [1] *batillementis* super turrim, continet in longitudine 17 gressus, et de novo edificata fuit cum ecclesia Sancti Johannis per Walterum Frampton nobilem mercatorem villæ Bristoll.*

[1] "Pinnacles."

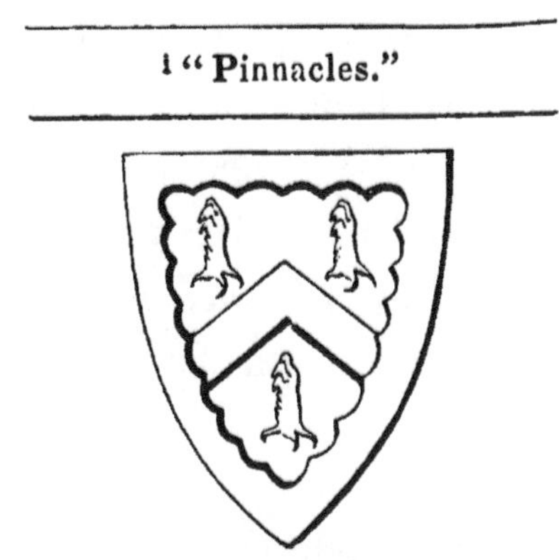

* **Frampton.**

Argent a cheveron between three Lions' jambs erased, within a bordure engrailed, gules.

Descent of Fromton or Frampton, from Wills and Deeds.

Walter Frampton, = the Founder of St. John Baptist's Church, buried there 1357, 30. Edw. iij.

Walter Frampton. = Isabel, daughter of
Will dated 1388, bur. in St. John's.

Robert =
Walter, a priest.

Walter Frampton. = Joan, daughter of
Will dated 1394,

Walter Frampton. = Alice, daughter of
Will dated 1423,

Richard, noticed in the Will.

Ecclesia Sancti Bartholomei, quondam prioratus canonicorum regularium per antecessores domini de le Warre fundata, et modo hospitale pauperum annui valoris . . . . . est scita prope et extra portas vocatas Frome-yate, in boriali parte villæ Bristoll.

Via a porta introitûs ad castellum Bristolliæ prope ecclesiam orientalem Sancti Petri, et sic eundo et gradiendo per murum fossi murorum castri per portam Newgate, et per vicum vocatum le Weere, et per pontem de le Weere, [k]*dimittendo* le wateryng-place in manu sinistra, et [l]*girando* per dictum murum fossi versus meridiem prope crucem de le market, sic continuando usque magnam petram de frestone unius virgæ erectam ad extremam libertatis franchesiæ villæ Bristolliæ in altera parte gardinorum Willelmi Worcestre ad portam primi introitus castri ex parte occidentali ecclesiæ Sancti Philippi,quæ est ad finem [m]*venellæ retro viæ mercati,* continet in circuitu unius partis turris et murorum castri 420 gressus.

Via quasi trianguli ab origine anguli pontis Bristoll. in opposita parte porti Sancti Nicholai ad principium de le bak, ubi unica domus aquæ conductûs 9 pedum longitudinis scituatur, continet 30 gressus; et a predicto angulo pontis Bristolliæ ad principium portæ Sancti Nicholai, quæ est pars dictæ viæ triangularis continet 14 gressus ; et a domo conducti de frestone, qui est conductus aquarum in principio de le bakk, eundo per ecclesiam [n]*de le crowd* Sancti Nicholai ad portam Sancti Nicholai.

---

[k] passing by, or leaving behind. [l] turning round. [m] "A lane at the back of the Old Market." [n] "The Crypt under the Church."

Via a dicta domo aquæ conductus eundo per le bak coram aqua de Avyn usque ad portam de Mersh-yate, par le crane et per orientalem partem capellæ T. Knappe* continet 270 gressus.

Portæ duæ cum archu desuper super extremam occidentalem capellæ Sanctæ Mariæ pontis,† continet longitudo inter primum murum archuatus, dicto muro archus computato cum vacua placea coram hostium capellæ, ad alteram portam °*peti archuati* cum muro dicti archuati computato continet 9 virgas sive 16 gressus.

° "Petræ archuatæ," of arched stone.

* **Knappe.**

Argent, a cross formee between four roses, gules.

† There were few very large bridges which had not a chapel erected upon them, as at London and York. This was of beautiful architecture and proportions, and had, independently of Elias Spelley's foundation of it, several legacies for the support of a Chantry, dedicated to the Assumption of the Virgin Mary. After the dissolution, this chapel was used as a warehouse, and was greatly damaged by a fire, February 7, 1646, when 24 houses towards St. Nicholas Church were burned down. The chapel had been previously desecrated by Walter Stephens, a leader of the Parliament party, after the surrender of the city in 1645. *M.S. Calendar.*

Latitudo tocius pontis, ut potest probari per spacium viæ pontis latitudinis inter dictas duas portas continet 5 virgas.

Latitudo viæ ad finem meridionalem pontis ad primum introitum longæ viæ de Radclyff-strete continet 5 virgas sive 8 gressus.

Market-place.

Via longa in posteriore parte [p]*a retro viæ de old Market* usque Lafford-yate : via posterior ex parte meridionali a retro de antiquo market, incipiendo a porta prima castri Bristoll. et transeundo per tria gardina Willelmi Worcestre in meridionali de le crosse in mercato predicto, sic transiens per longam viam juxta cimiterium et ecclesiam Sancti Philippi, ubi quondam ecclesia religiosorum et prioratus in orientali parte ecclesiæ Sancti Philippi scituatur, et sic continue eundo a retro gardina tenementorum in mercato antiquo usque ad murum ecclesiæ occidentalem ecclesiæ hospitalis Sanctæ Trinitatis per venerabilissimum mercatorem quondam villæ Bristoll. ad dictam ecclesiam Sanctæ Trinitatis per Johannem Barstaple* fundatum et edificatum pro XIII hominibus pauperibus, continet in longitudine 660 gressus.

Hospitale domûs cum capellâ in veteri mercato prope Laffords yate cum capella condecenti per dictum Barstaple est fundata et erecta.

---

p "behind the road of the Old Market."

---

* In the floor of the Hospital Chapel, are inserted two large and well wrought Brasses, representing a man in the dress of a burgess, with a belt and basilard, or short dagger, and his wife in the female dress of the times. Inscriptions :—

Porta Laffordys-yate per dictum Walterum Barstaple de novo fundata et composita tempore regis Edwardi tertii, vel Ricardi regis secundi, ubi finis libertas et franchesiæ villæ Bristolliæ in hoc termino occidentali extendit ad quandam petram altitudinis unius virgæ extra Laffordys-yate erectam in parte boriali dictæ portæ, per me visam et palpatam.

Altitudo dictæ portæ super pulcram mansionem desuper edificatam . . . .

Viæ longitudo ab exteriori parte Laffordys-yate,

"Hic jacet Johannes Barstaple, burgensis villae Bristol. fundator istius loci, qui obijt 15 kalen. Octob. litera Dominicalis, D. A.D. MCCCCXL., cujus animae propitietur Deus. Amen."

"Hic jacet Isabella quond. uxor. Johannis Barstaple, quae obijt. A.D. DCCCC., cujus animae propitietur Deus. Amen."

Barstaple.

Descent of Barstaple, from Wills.

John Barstaple, ob. 1410, Founder of the Hospital at Lawford's Gate = Isabel, daughter of Walter Darby, ob. 1400.

- Thomas
- John
- Nicholas, first Master of the Hospital, founded by his father.
- Joan = Robert Shipward.
  - William Shipward, "aliter dictus Barstaple." Will dated 1467.

continuando usque ad ecclesiam et domum ac hospitale pertinenti dictæ ecclesiæ, continet in longitudine in comitatu Gloucestriæ incipiente, et versus viagium ad civitatem Londoniarum transeuncium per forestam de Kyngyswod, incipiente apud Laffordys-yate continet usque dictum hospitalem Sancti Laurencii* per . . . . fundatam, quamvis modo pertinet tempore Edwardi regis quarti collegio et ecclesiæ de Westbery, 1200 gressus per W. Worcestre mensuratis.

Via magna prope Laffordys-yate in parte boriali dictæ portæ juxta le meerestone finis libertatis Bristolliæ; ac via magna in parte boriali similiter non multum longæ, qua itur et revertitur in parte et clima boriali extra Laffordys-yate, eundo et equitando per . . . . ad villam Gloucetyr per villas Wynterborn, Tyderynton, Newport . . . . usque Gloucestre per spacium 30 miliariorum distans a Bristollia.

Le Market-weyes usque Lafford-yate.

Via non edificata in altera parte boriali de le market-place in parochia Sancti Philippi.

Via longa incipiente ad finem viæ de le weere ex altera parte viæ, ubi equi Bristolliæ consueverunt bibere in angulo cornerii meridionali dicti wateryng-place, et sic continuando viam usque domum hospitalis Sanctæ Trinitatis fundatam per Walterum Barstaple prope Laffordys-yate, et ex transverso viæ veniente de le [q] *veyle market* usque [r] *milliam*

[q] Old Market. [r] "Molendinum."

* Hospital of St. Laurence belonging to the College of Westbury, t. Edw. 4ti.; built by Walter Barstaple, the father of John, who founded the Hospital.

quondam Walteri Carillton, continet in longitudine cum viæ retornæ versus et prope hospitalem Sanctæ Trinitatis ad viam de market prope Laffordys-yate 569 gressus.

Latitudo dictæ viæ per majorem partem continet . . . . per estimacionem, sed non est edificata nisi per longitudinem . . . . gressuum citra le wateryng-place de le Weer, sed in latitudine circa . . . . gressus.

Venella prope ecclesiam Sancti Philippi, ducens de le style cimeterii dictæ ecclesiæ directe per le travers de dicto market, continet 77 gressus.

Latitudo ejusdem venellæ de petrâ non edificata, continet 7 virgas.

Venella alia ducens directe de illa priori venella ex transverso de le market, transiens ad borialem viam sive partem per le magnum gardinum et orchard Markyswilliam* majoris quondam villæ Bristolliæ ad aquam de Frome, ultra le wateryngplace de le Weere, versus Erlysmede, continet 136 gressus.

[s] *Via lapidea longa et lata*, vocata le veile market,

---

[s] "A highway pitched or paved with stones."

---

* The true name of this person was Mac William, of whom *Leland* has given the following account:—*Itin. v.* 8. *p.* 97. "One Mac Williams being the younger son of a gentilman in Ireland, came to Bristowe, and ther so increased in riches, that he bought landes to the sum of three or four hundred markes by the yere, and so the land contynued a certein while, in the heirs male of Mac Williams, and after cam to a dawter of theirs, that was married to one of the Seymours." Sir John Seymour, in 1430, possessed several houses and messuages in Redcliff-street, (see Deeds) probably so inherited.

a principio altæ crucis prope fossam castro Bristoll. directe eundo per quatuor tenementa Willelmi Worcestre ad Laffordes-yate scita, ut media et principalis via duarum aliarum longarum viarum, una ex parte meridionali et alia via ex parte boriali, continet 660 gressus.

Latitudo dictæ viæ continet 54 gressus.

Via eundo ad prioratum montis acuti* Sancti Jacobi per le justyng-place ab antiquis diebus.

Via in parochia Sancti Jacobi in occidentali parte ecclesiæ Sancti Jacobi prope portam principalem introitus ad prioratum Sancti Jacobi, et partem muri orientalem fratrum Sancti Francisci.

Via longa, sive venella, de fine viæ Lewenysmede ex opposito cimiterii Sancti Jacobi, eundo per hostium prioris religionum dictæ ecclesiæ, et sic continuando ad extremam partem dictæ viæ sive venellæ per muros gardinorum fratrum Sancti Francisci ad quendam montem acutum in boriali parte dictæ viæ extrema, et retornando per aliud retornum viæ ducentis versus montem ecclesiæ Sancti Michaelis,

* The King's down was so called, as having been part of the demesne lands connected with the Castle, and frequented for exercise, both by the soldiers and inhabitants. This part of the King's down, still retaining the name of Montacute or Montagu, was from the time of the establishment of martial exercises for the soldiers of the garrison, continued till a late period, for such purposes. Marshal-street (now corrupted to Merchant-street) was the military way leading to it from the Castle. In the accounts of T. Lord Berkeley is an entry—"for spere-play at Bristow;" and the expense of these joustings or hastiludes was borne by a contribution of the inhabitants, at certain periods, after the garrison had been withdrawn.

continet dicta via sive venella erecta 300 gressus. Et [t]*retornum* dictæ viæ ad partem orientalem per murum dictorum fratrum minorum usque ad venellam eundo ad ecclesiam Sancti Michaelis, et sic continuando directe orientaliter usque ad altam crucem petræ erectæ de frestone cum fonte clausa de frestone ad altiorem finem viæ veniente de ecclesia Sancti Bartholomei vocatum Stype-strete, continet 600 gressus.

Memorandum quod ad dictam crucem obviant 3 viæ, quarum una vocatur Stanley ducens ad villam Clyfton, vel ad viam ducentem usque Ghyston-clyff.

Latitudo ejus continet 4 virgas prope [u]*conductorium* . . . . . de frestone in meridionali parte dictæ portæ scituat.

Via vocata Marchalle strete in parochia Sancti Jacobi, videlicet a fine viæ Brodemede prope pontem muri fratrum predicatorum, eundo versus cimiterium Sancti Jacobi per lez barrys ubi mulieres fatuæ morantur* usque ad angulum cornerii intrando ad prioratum . . . . Sancti Jacobi per unum mulbery-tree, continet 191 gressus.

Latitudo dictæ viæ per tenementa mea Willelmi Worcestre . . . . . .

Via proxima sequens, videlicet ab angulo cornerii, eundo versus Redelyngton† per le mulbery-tree superius nominatum, et sic eundo versus cimiterium Sancti Jacobi usque ad introitum primum ecclesiæ predictæ, continet 155 gressus; et sic

---

[t] "the return." [u] "the Conduit."

---

* The public stews. † Now Redland.

continuando [w]*per costeram* cimiterii Sancti Jacobi usque crucem et pontem occidentalem dictæ viæ ad returnum viæ vocatæ le Bak ad finem occidentalem cimiterii predicti, ubi una porta cum [x]*uno stilo petræ* scituatur, continet 240 gressus; et sic in toto longitudo dictæ viæ continet 395 gressus.

Latitudo dictæ viæ ex una parte edificatæ continet . . . gressus.

Latitudo viæ de le bak in parochia Sancti Nicholai continet 34 gressus.

Latitudo secundæ viæ gradus, voc. anglice [y]*le slep*, qui est proximior ad introitum Baldwyn-strete continet 4 virgas.

Volta archus sanctæ crucis* et ecclesiæ Sancti Johannis continet in longitudine circa 60 gressus.

Latitudo dictæ voltæ sive archus 13 gressus.

Key: longitudo a prima incepcione coram muro templi Judér† prope portam petram introitus Smalstrete usque angulum domus de petrâ muro fortissimo edificato ex opposito abbathiæ Sancti Augustini continet per aquam de Frome et calcetum de le key 480 gressus bene computatos.

Longitudo ecclesiæ Seynt Ewen, id est Sancti Adoen, continet 22 virgas.

Latitudo dictæ ecclesiæ, cujus orientalis pars altaris est directe ex opposito ecclesiæ sanctæ tri

---

w "by the side of." x "a stone stile." y "the Slip."

---

* The Crypt, dedicated to the Holy Cross, under St. John Baptist's Church: as that under St. Nicholas to the Virgin Mary.—"*B. M. Virgini.*"

† Templi Judæorum, the ancient Synagogue.

nitatis prope crucem Bristolliæ, continet 15 virgas per mensuratas vel 30 gressus.

Et habet unam navem ecclesiæ ex parte boriali alæ, et unam [z]*alam vel elam*, quæ est capella Sancti Johannis Baptistæ, et fraternitatis.

Ecclesiæ longitudo omnium sanctorum directe ex opposito ecclesiæ . . . . . continet . . . gressus, vel tot. 23 virgas.

Latitudo dictæ ecclesiæ continet 20 virgas sive 34 gressus.

Longitudo ecclesiæ predictæ Sanctæ Trinitatis 22 virgas.

Latitudo ecclesiæ Sanctæ Trinitatis 35 gressus.

Latitudo viæ Hygh-strete ad altam crucem 24 gressus.

Latitudo viæ de Wynch-strete ad altam viam 16 gressus.

Longitudo viæ vocatæ Bradstrete continet 328 gressus.

Latitudo viæ de Bradstrete ad altam crucem 14 gressus.

Sed ejus latitudo in medio viæ Bradstrete 24 gressus.

Latitudo viæ de Corne-strete ad altam crucem 14 gressus.

Latitudo domus Willelmi Botoner 15 gressus.

Latitudo domus [a]*Gylhalde* cum capella Sancti Georgii 40 gressus.

Longitudo voltæ [b]*Sancti Johannis constat ex sex archuatis, cum 6 fenestris in una costera versus bo-*

[z] "The Aisle." [a] "Guildhall." [b] "St. John's church has six bays or arches, with six windows on the North side, and two only on the South." "Frettè—vowted," with recessed arches, richly pannelled."

riam, et duabus fenestris versus meridiem frette vowted.

Volta Sancti Johannis Baptistæ est in alto 16 steppys sive gradus,* et quilibet gradus continet 8 pollices.

Via vocata le through-hows in meridionali viæ de Wynch-strete per Haddon-tanerie† ad vicum Seynt Mary port-strete continet in longitudine 90 gressus,

Latitudo ejus continet 4 gressus in medio viæ.

Venella apud signum le swan‡ in Wynch-strete transiens ad vicum vocatum Seynt Mary port continet circa 90 gressus.

Latitudo viæ Wynch-strete in medio continet 22 gressus.

Vicus transiens de Wynch-strete ad vicum vocatum Seynt Peter strete ex opposito fontis de frestone prope ecclesiam Sancti Petri continet 80 gressus.

Via de Newgate ad pontem de le Weere prope

* The step or gradus, when applied to height, is eight inches each—when to distance is twenty inches: gradus and gressus are used distinctly.

† Inscription in All Saints' church—"Hic requiescunt corpora bonæ memoriæ Johannis Haddon, vyntner et Christinæ uxoris sue. Qui obijt. 11 die martij, A.D. 1434. Quorum animabus propicietur Deus! Amen."

‡ The Swan ducally gorged and chained, as always exhibited on signs for hostels or inns, was the cognizance of the Bohuns, Earls of Hereford, and from them of King Henry 4th, and Stafford, Duke of Buckingham. The nobility had their hostels in their provincial towns, and this probably belonged to the Duke of Buckingham.

le wateryng place ad quendam petram magnam prope murum de dyke continet 360 gressus.

[c] *Via proxima contermina de predicta ponte in fine de Weere,* et petræ magnæ ad altam crucem de le market, transeundo ex opposito tenementorum Willelmi Worcestre continet 300 gressus.

Via longa a sancta cruce ad portas Laffordysyate continet 600 gressus, vocata le market, per ecclesiam hospitalis Barstaple fundatam in honore Sanctæ Trinitatis.

Castri orientalis partis muri profundi fossi a porta et angulo orientali, a porta prope finem occidentalem cimiterii ecclesiæ Sancti Philippi, continuando per fossam muri usque ad angulum orientalem pontis de Were, [d]*et sic girando per pontem molendinorum prope Newgate** et transeundo per primam portam Newgate usque ad introitum portæ fossi profundi [e]*ad valvas introitus castri,* continet sepcies 360 gressus, qui faciunt circa 2100 gressus.

Avyn-mersh.

Circumferentia marisci XII brachia, ut relatum mihi per unum rope-maker.

Longitudo de le slip, anglice [f]*a steyre,* de lapidibus ad fundum aquæ de le bak, id est a summi-

---

[c] "The next road which terminates at the bridge aforesaid, at the end of the Wear." [d] "And so turning over the bridge of the Mills near Newgate." [e] "The great Gates of entrance into the Castle," which nearly fronted the East end of St. Peter's church. [f] "A stair" or flight of steps.

---

* These were the great Corn-Mills upon the river Froom, which severally belonged to the Castle and the Town.

tate viæ desuper le bak usque ad ultimum gradum continencium descensu 920 gressus.

Latitudo dictæ gradus ad fundum aquæ continet 10 virgas, id est 40 pedes.

Altitudo de fundo aquæ Avonæ ad finem dictæ gradus, anglice a steyr, continet circa 7 brachia vel 6 brachia.

Latitudo viæ vocatæ Corne-strete* ad finem portæ Sancti Leonardi 24 gressus.

Edificacio quadrata, vocata le rakhyth in occidentali parte capellæ Thomæ Knap super le bak scitæ, unum quadratum a [g]*boria in meridiem* 50 gressus, et ab oriente in occidentem 40 gressus.

Via sive venella, quæ ducit ab hostio de rakhyth ad le bak per meridionalem partem cimiterii capellæ Thomæ Knapp, continet circa 80 gressus.

Via sive venella, quæ incipit in parte boriali ecclesiæ Sancti Nicholai de le porta ejus sive de fine Hygh-strete ducens ad viam sive venellam descensûs gradus 30 ad Baldwyne-strete ex opposito crucis, continet de principio dicti gradûs 124 gressus.

Et sic continuando dictam viam usque portam Sancti Leonardi continet circa 300 gressus.

Longitudo navis ecclesiæ Sancti Leonardi† continet 12 virgas, cum choro 7 virgæ, 19 virgæ circa 30 gressus.

Latitudo ejus continet 10 virgas.

---

[g] "From North to South."

---

* Called in Deeds Old Corne-Street.

† Taken down with the gate-way under the Tower in 1771, when Clare-Street was built.

Viæ latitudo a fine venellæ ducentis de porta Sancti Leonardi, viz., a principio domus de le custom-hows usque venellam ab hospicio . . . . Shyppard* ad introitum venellæ eundo ad occidentalem partem campanilis Sancti Stephani continet 70 gressus.

Venella parva supra-nominata, eundo ad ecclesiam Sancti Stephani per orientalem partem ecclesiæ Sancti Stephani et altaris principalis ecclesiæ predictæ, continet 80 gressus.

Latitudo viæ de le key ex parte de le custom-hows usque directe eundo ad quandam venellam, incipiendo [h] *a retro domus Shyppard*, eundo ad portam occidentalem ecclesiæ Sancti Stephani 34 gressus, versus locum apertum partis de le key, ubi in medio conductus aquæ de petra frestone scituatur.

Venella proxima adjuncta, eundo per le stile per

---

h "The back of Shyppard's house.

---

* In Wyrcestre's time there were several very large and handsome houses belonging to the more opulent inhabitants, which he has particularised :—

1. Shipward's; near St. Stephen's Church.
2. Canynges; in Redcliffe Street.
3. Norton's; behind St. Peter's Church.
4. Olyver's; in Wynch Street.
5. Bagod's; upon the Town Wall, and in a tower rebuilt by Clement Bagod, near the Grey Friars' Church.
6. Pavye's; near St. Giles's Church, Small Street.
7. Pownham's; Lewin's Mead.
8. Vyell's place; on the Quay beyond the Marsh-gate.
9. Newton (the Recorder's); in Castle Street, opposite to St. Peter's porch.
10. Sturmye's; upon the Welsh Bec.

cimiterium, incipiendo ab orientali parte ecclesiæ Sancti Stephani, et sic directe eundo per meridionalem partem cimiterii dictæ ecclesiæ usque le key, continet cum 30 gressibus per cimiterium predictum, et tunc directe transeundo per occidentalem partem ecclesiæ predictæ ad locum vocatum le key continet 90 gressus, sed [1]*equi havers* non transeunt per dictam venellam.

De operacione artificiosa porticus borialis ecclesiæ Sancti Stephani de opere manuali Benet le freemason.*†

A cors wythout.(1)‡
A casement.(2)
A bowtelle.(3)
A felet.(4)

---

[1] "Equi halliers," horses drawing sledges.

---

* There is no porch on the North side of the Church. "Portam *meridionalem* ecclesiæ de novo factam." See page 38. The South is evidently described. It has been lately restored, but imperfectly, for the modern battlements have been retained. This very minute and workmanlike account was doubtless communicated to William Wyrcestre, by Norton, the master mason of Redcliff, subsequently mentioned.

† The French term *Frère Maçon* has been anglicized into *Free-Mason;* and refers not to their immunities, but to their Gild or Fraternity.

‡ Masonic terms in the 15th Century :—

1. A basement or plinth immediately above ground.
2. A moulding deeply hollowed.
3. Boltellus. Boutel. A perpendicular shaft attached to a pillar.
4. A narrow flat moulding.

A double ressaunt. (5)
A boutel.
A felet.
A ressaunt.
A felde.
A casement wyth levys. (6)
A felet.
A boutel.
A felet.
A ressant.
A felet.
A casement wyth trayles f.(7)
A felet.
A boutel.
A felet.
A casement.
A felet.
A casement.
A felet.
In the myddes of the dore a battelle. (8)

Ecclesia de Radclyff.

* Longitudo tocius ecclesiæ Beatæ Mariæ de Radclyff continet 63 virgas præter capellam Beatæ Mariæ.

5. Now called an ogee moulding, either double or single.
6. A moulding formed of curved foils, rosettes, or leaves, sometimes with crockets.
7. A casement with Trefoils, exactly resembling a window closed, in the solid wall.
8. This term sometimes means battlement, but it does not apply in this instance. Perhaps it may mean here the arch formed by three quarter open circles conjoined, after the Burgundian manner.

* From page 82 of Nasmith's Edition.

Longitudo capellæ Beatæ Mariæ 13 virgæ 1 pes et dimidium.

Latitudo capellæ 7 virgæ.

Latitudo ecclesiæ tocius 18 virgæ.

Summa tocius longitudinis continet 77 virgas.

Longitudo secundariæ portæ ex parte boriali 7 virgæ.

Latitudo dictæ porchæ 4 virgæ et quarta pars.

Longitudo de crosse-isles 38 virgæ.

Latitudo trium elarum voltarum cum lapidibus 14 virgas continet.

Latitudo cujuslibet arcûs infra columpnas, continet 10 pedes.

Longitudo de le crosse-isle continet 8 arcus a boria in meridiem.

Et quælibet fenestra in le ovyrstorye continet 5 panellas.

Et quælibet fenestra in latitudine continet 10 pedes.

Et quælibet fenestra finis cujuslibet elæ continet 3 panellas vitreatas.*

Turris ecclesiæ Radclyff in longitudine continet 23 pedes dimid. et in latitudine 24 pedes.

Altitudo turris continet 120 pedes, et altitudo de le spere sicut modo fracta continet 200 pedes.†

Et diameter in superiori fracturæ continet 16 pedes.

* "*Panellæ vitreatæ,*" divisions of a window composed of stained glass, in distinction to common glass. The word is so used by William Wyrcestre, and elsewhere, "Panella glasatta," are merely glased windows.

† Meaning 200 feet of total elevation.

Et habet 8 pannas.*

Et quilibet lapis in incepcione speræ continet in densitate duos pedes; et apud [j] *le topp* in altiori parte ubi crux scituatur, continet densitudo 4 pollices; et quilibet lapis in fabricacione est 8 pedes latitudinis . . . . in densitudine; et latitudo de le garlond† continet XI pedes.

Densitudo murorum turris de Radclyff in fundamento 7 pedes.

Et in altitudine 120 pedum continet murus 5 pedes.

Longitudo primæ portæ porticus ecclesiæ Beatæ Mariæ côntinet 7 virgas, et capella continuata ad portam introitus portæ ecclesiæ principalis continet 6 virgas.

Latitudo dictæ capellæ continet 5 virgas.‡

Turris campanarum ecclesiæ Sancti Jacobi ab boria in meridiem continet 6 virgas.

Et ab oriente in occidentem 5 virgas.

Ecclesia Sancti Audoeni in latitudine 14 virgas.

Latitudo ecclesiæ Sanctæ Trinitatis continet 32 gressus.

---

j "At the summit."

---

* Panes or segments of the Spire inclosed within ribs.

† The ballustrade which surrounds the broken spire.

‡ Dimensions of Redcliff Church according to Barrett's History of Bristol, p. 573. Total length 239 feet; Transept 117=44; Breadth of Transept and side isles, 59; Height of ailes, 25 feet; Nave, 54; and the transept of equal height; Nave from the West end to the high Altar, 197: Our Lady's Chapel 42=24, and 26 feet high.

Longitudo ecclesiæ Sanctæ Trinitatis continet 22 virgas.

Latitudo ecclesiæ Sanctæ Werburgæ continet . . . .

Ecclesia Sancti Petri continet in longitudine preter chorum 54 gressus.

Latitudo ejus continet 30 gressus.

Ecclesia Sanctæ Mariæ de la port continet preter chorum in longitudine 27 gressus.

1469 Mr. Robertus Lane* obiit, grammaticus villæ Bristoll. die 23 febr.

Longitudo navis ecclesiæ de Radclyff continet 13 archus altos cum 3 fenestris desuper le ovyrstorye, et quælibet fenestra habet 5 panes altitudinis 12 pedum, et latitudinis 4 virgarum vitreatarum sic in toto. Et quælibet fenestra continet 4 virgas latitudinis, et habet 5 panys vitreatas quælibet fenestra: sed in duabus alis ecclesiæ quælibet fenestra non habet nisi quatuor panellas vitreatas.

Ghyston-clyff.

Breke faucet est subtus Ghyston-clyff apud Lymotes sub valle Brandon-hille.

Fons calidus emanet de profundo aquæ Avyn, sicut est Bathoniæ, in le rok de Gyston-clyff, in eadem parte in le shole-place.

Scarlet-welle est directe in parte opposita, in alta parte de Hungrode, emanente de rupe.

[k]*Ledes est unus rokk under Gynston-clyff, a dan-*

---

[k] "Ledes is a rock under Ghystone-Cliff, and there is danger if a ship comes to enter Bristol, that is, too hastily over these stones; or if it delays too long, the tide makes it dangerous to hoist a sail, on account of the rocks, which lie at the bottom of the course of the river, under Ghystone-Cliff."

ger si venit et intrat Bristolliæ, id est nimis tempestive ovyrstone, et si diu tardat fluxum maris est periculosus ad velandum pro rupibus jacentibus in fundo maris cursus de Gyston-clyff.

Brandon-hylle* in Hibernia scita est; altissimus mons tocius Hiberniæ ultra Blasquey in occidentalissima parte tocius Hiberniæ; et ibi sunt lapides vocat cristalle-stonys.

A porta Sancti Leonardi viæ de Baldwin-stret usque le custom-hous.

Latitudo viæ ibidem 5 virgæ ad angulum trianguli de le custom-hous incipiente.

Corne-strete continet 17 cellaria in parte omnium sanctorum.

Via de Hygh-strete in parte posteriori ecclesiæ omnium sanctorum continet 60 gressus.

Latitudo dictæ viæ continet unam virgam.

Latitudo parvæ viæ omnium sanctorum a retro occidentalis ecclesiæ 5 virgæ.

In via predicta parva est unum cellarium pro vino.

Naves Bristolliæ pertinentes in anno Christi 1480.

Mary Grace 300 doliata.

Le . . 360 doliata.†

* See the *Legend of St. Brendane*, an Irish saint, who was likewise said to have been a giant, printed by W. de Worde.

† That ships of so great a burthen could, at that time, have been received into the Port of Bristol, may admit of doubt. I have been informed by an intelligent friend, that it is probable that ships, here said to have been 360 tons, did not, as to their actual burthen, exceed one-half of that tonnage at present, (1480—1830.) Ships as now con-

George 200 doliata.
Kateryn 180 dol.
Mary Bryd 100 dol.
Cristofer 90 dol.
Mary Shernman 54 doliat.
Leonard 50 Tontyghe.
Mary of Bristowe . . lex.
Le George qui quer . . Johannes 511 tonne.
. . . navis, qui dispositus est ad mare.
Johannes Godeman* habet navium . .
Thomas† Straunge circiter XII.

Pons Bristoll.

Altitudo turris quadratæ campanilæ in sinistra capellæ edificatæ de petra ab area continet ad cameram campanarum 15 brachia et per cordas campanarum mensuratas, et altissima camera continet in altitudine circa tria brachia, sic in tota altitudine circa 18 brachia.

structed, measuring 500 tons, will in fact convey 800 or 900 tons. Whereas, it is strictly probable, that those mentioned in this list, or those belonging to W. Canynges, would not have borne a burthen equal to their measurement.

"Although the greater ships had English names, there is a doubt whether we had ships of that size of our own building. Canynges might have taken or purchased them from the Venetians, Hanseatics, or Genoese, all of whom had ships of even a larger burthen at that time."—*Anderson's Hist. of Commerce*, V. 1., p. 271.

* John Godeman does not occur as holding any municipal office.

† Quære Robert? The family of Strange was one of the most opulent of the merchants. Robert Strange was Mayor 1483, and Burgess in Parliament 1484.

Longitudo pontis prædictæ continet 94 gressus.*

Memorandum quod Helyas Spelly burgensis villæ Bristoll. est, et fuit cum . . . .
. . . .
majores benefactores capellæ predictæ, ut patet in fenestris vitreatis cum figura eorum et uxorum suarum in dictis fenestris, videlicet Helyas Spelly.†

1446. Memorandum quod mense julii ante festum Sancti Jacobi, Robertus Sturmyn mercator villæ Bristolliæ incepit viagium suum de porta Bristoll. a Kyngrode ad Jerusalem cum circa 160 peregrinis, et navigando per Cyville, eundo ad portam Joppa et Jerusalem; et in redeundo versus Angliam per Modon insulam‡ ex subita procella et forti vento orto in atrâ et obscurâ nocte 23 diei Decembris incaute ex improviso navis ejus vocata le Cogg-Anne ad rupem et terram prostrata fuit, et 37 homines et marinarii submersi fuerunt in maximum dolorem amicorum eorum Bristolliæ et eorum uxorum. Sed quidam devotus episcopus de Modon in Grecia fecit corpora mortuorum 37 predictorum honorifice sepeliri, et fundavit sanctam

* The height of the tower of the chapel of St. Mary on the Bridge:—From the area of the bridge to the summit of the belfry, 90 feet; to the top of the tower, 18 feet; total, 108 feet.

† This very slight notice of stained glass windows, with portraits of benefactors, is the only one which occurs in the whole of Wyrcestre's survey. Such must, in his day, have abounded in the churches of Bristol, but he was too intent upon measuring floors, to raise his vision to the gorgeous windows, or they were too frequent to attract his minute observation.

‡ *Modon* lies on the Continent.

capellam de nova ibidem ad orandum pro animabus eorum et omnium fidelium defunctorum.

Longitudo sive spacium viæ apud le bak in parochia Sancti Nicholai erga capellam de le bakk continet 50 gressus apud Crane.

Gradus primus, anglice a slypp, super le bak de aqua Avyn, proxima vico vocato Baldewyne-strete continet in longitudine ad fundum aquæ Avenæ ascendendo ad altum vicum de le bak 80 gradus, anglice steyres.

Gradus secundus, anglice a slypp, proxime sequens in dicto vico de le bak, propinqua capellæ Sancti Johannis Evangelistæ, continet in longitudine circa 80 gressus.

Latitudo duorum longorum graduum de le bak usque fundum aquæ de Avyn, ubi mulieres lavant pannas lineos, aliquando 12 mulieres simul ad pedem aquæ de Avyn lavantes pannos lineos et alia necessaria vidi; ut mulieres honestæ* sic ibidem

* In distinction from mulieres fatuæ before mentioned— "Honestæ et fatuæ mulieres," are discriminated by William Wyrcestre, but in the ancient ordinances of the Camps, their female followers were called "Lotrices and Meretrices," with the same meaning.

This publick "Lavanderie" is still practised at Paris, in the Seine. These slips or stone-stairs from the Bec to the river, were of infinite accommodation to the female inhabitants of this most closely compacted town, with so dense a population, as it then inclosed, within its walls. The river, even in the reflux of the tide, must have been never "clara et pura," but fit only for certain domestic uses. Bristol was not deficient in public wells and fountains, brought by leaden pipes into castellets or receptacles of stone, as mentioned by *Leland* distinctly.

quando fluxus maris returnat versus mare, et quod aqua Avyn veniente a porta Bristolliæ sit clara et pura, sic lavant certis temporibus diei.

Naves naviculæ et cimbæ, ac naviculæ vocatæ anglice wodbryshys cachecys pycardes, venientes de portubus villarum Walliæ; sunt de villis et havyns de Tynby, Myllford-havyn, West Herford, Lawgher-havyn, Lanstefan-havyn, Kedwelly-havyn, Swansley-havyn, Neth-havyn, Kerdyff-havyn, Newport-havyn, Wsque-havyn, Kerlyon-havyn, Tyntern monasterium super flumen de Wye, Chepstow-havyn, Betysley-water super aquam de Wy, et aliæ portus sive hamones de comitatibus et portubus Cornwalliæ, oneratis cum stangno piscibus etcæt, ac de portubus de Devynshyre, Somersetshyre, applicant cum eorum navibus ad le bak ad exonerandas et discarcandas eorum naves de eorum mercandisis.

Capella decens, longitudinis . . virgarum . . . . . . super le bak Bristolliæ prope Mershyate est edificatum per venerabilem mercatorem cognominatum Knapp, pro duobus capellanis sustinendis in terris et tenementis, ita quod semper omni die, horâ v in mane, illi, vel unus dictorum suorum capellanorum, dicent missam pro mercatoribus marinariis et artificis ac servientibus, possunt adire ad audiendas missas tempore matutinali.*

* This chapel stood on the Welch Back, near the Marsh gate. The Irish and Spanish sailors were bound to hear mass and present offerings, at the Chapels of St. Vincent and St. Brendane, when they came into the harbour. Those who sailed in the Bristol Channel, at the Chapel of St. Blaise, upon a hill in the parish of Henbury.

Le crane, officium instrumenti, super le bak est scitum, prope portam vocatam le mersh-yate, bene fundatum et fortiter in terra fixum.

Domus et hospicium pro communi utilitate villæ vocatum a cloth-halle est super le bak ordinatum, quondam Roberti Sturmyn* venerabilis mercatoris villæ Bristoll. manentis et hospicium amplum custodientis tam pro externis mercatoribus quam aliis generosis.

* Sturmye.

Argent—3 Gryphen's heads erased gules.

The cloth hall upon the Welch Back was part of the mansion house of Robert Sturmye, Mayor in 1450, and the most hospitable of merchants, who kept there an open table, daily, for foreign merchants and the gentlemen of Bristol, to the great benefit of commerce, then first assuming its present system. Sturmye's hospitable reception of the foreign merchants who frequented or resided in Bristol, affords proof that the commercial intercourse with other nations was then considerable.

36 Hen. 6. (1458). "In this year, after some auctors, a merchant of Bristowe, named Sturmye, which with his ship had travailed in divers parts of the Levaunt and other parts of the Est, for so much as the fame ranne upon him, that he had gotten some green pepper and other spyces to have sette and sown in Englande as the fame went, therefore the Janawayes (Genoese) wayted him upon the sea and spoiled his ship and another. But this is full like to be

Ecclesia parochialis Sancti Audoeni cum capella fraternitatis in honore Sancti Johannis Baptistæ* scita directâ lineâ inter ecclesiam Sanctæ Werburgæ ex parte occidentali et vicum vocatum Bradstrete ex parte orientali; et magna fenestra orientalis altaris dictæ ecclesiæ scita super stratum Bradstrete.

Ecclesia parochialis Sanctæ Trinitatis scita in directâ lineâ ecclesiæ Audoeni ex parte occidentali dictæ ecclesiæ; ac [1]*buttat* super orientali parte vici Bradstrete; et meridionalis pars dictæ ecclesiæ est scita cum porta ejusdem apud crucem altam in quadrivio de Bradstrete, Hygh-strete, Corn-strete, et Wynch-strete quondam Castel-stret; et dicta ecclesia habet turrim quadratam cum campanis ac speram altam cum lapidibus de frestone condecenter operatam.

---

[1] abuts.

---

untrue that the Januwayes should spoil him for any such cause; for there is no nacion in Europe that dealeth so little in spyces. But were it for this cause or other, the trouthe is, that by that nacion an offence was done for the which all the merchants Janawayes in London were arrested and sent to the Flete till they had found sufficient security to answer the premises. And finally for the harmys that theyr nacion had done to this Sturmye vi M. markes was sette to their payne to paye, but how it was paid, no mention I finde." *Fabyan's Chronicle.* Qto. (reprint), p. 663.

* This was a fraternity of Merchant Tailors, and was the largest and most opulent, composed of the tradesmen, in Bristol. St. John was the patron Saint.

Ecclesia parochialis omnium sanctorum scita super vicum Corn-strete in parte boriali, et prope crucem altam de Hygh-strete ex parte orientali, et habet turrim quadratam pro campanis pulsantibus.

Ecclesia parochialis Beatæ Mariæ de Radclyff in altera parte pontis Bristoll. super altum montem scituata, et edificata velut ecclesia cathedralis cum turri quadratâ largâ occupata cum . . campanis largæ quantitatis et ponderis.

Memorandum de navibus ad expensas Domini Wilelmi Canynghys, de novo fabricatis in villâ Bristolliæ.†*

Dominus Wilhelmus Canyngis qui fuit major, 5 vicibus, per octo annos exhibuit 800 homines in navibus occupatos, et habuit operarios et carpentarios, masons, &c. omni die C. homines.

De navibus habuit le Mary Canyngys de 400 doliatis.

* Canynges.

Argent—3 Moors heads erased proper boudest azure and argent.

† Inserted in page 99 of Nasmith's Edition. The ships supplied by Bristol to the armament in 1372, from the M.S. of W. de Ayrmine, Comptroller of Accounts, is published in *Seyer's Memoirs*, v. 2., p. 151. There were not more than two or three of 100 tons; and mostly of 40 or 50 tons.

Le Mary Radclyf pondere 500 doliatarum.

Le Mary et John pondere 900 doliatarum, constabat sibi in toto 4000 marcas.

Le Galyot navis pondere 50 doliatarum.

Le Cateryn pondere 140 doliatarum.

Le Marybat pondere 220 doliatarum.

Le Margyt de Tynly pondere 200 doliatarum.

Le lytylle Nicholas pondere 140 doliatarum.

Le Kateryn de Boston pondere 220 doliatarum.

Le . . . . navis in Iselond perdita, circa pondus 160 doliatarum.

Item, ultra ista, Edwardus Rex quartus habuit de dicto Wilhelmo III millia marcarum pro pace suâ habendâ.*

Ecclesia parochialis de sanctâ cruce, quondam ordinis templariorum in templo Jerusalem, modo de Sancto Johanne Baptistâ ordine in Jerosolimitana civitate primo ortâ et fundatâ, ac diebus modernis, ecclesia religiosorum ordinis præfatæ Johannis Baptistæ apud insulam de Rodes florente.

Et dicta ecclesia parochialis Bristolliæ in diocesi Bathoniensi et Wellensi super aquam de Avyn scituata in altera parte de Avyn.

Altitudo turris quadratæ de novo fabricatæ circa annum Christi 1460. per parochianos villæ pro campanis magnificis pulsandis et sonandis.

Capella Sancti Johannis Evangelistæ super le Bakk fundata per magnificum virum mercatorem et burgensem† Bristoll. scita super le . .

* For his acquittal in the Exchequer. Canynges was Mayor and King's Seneschal, and Chief Commissioner for the subsidy then levied.

† Thomas Knappe Mayor, 1403.

Capella pulcherrima cum voltâ larga et alta archuata cum lapidibus, subtus capellam Beatæ Mariæ Virginis super medium locum pontis Bristolliæ, ac super pontem fortissimum archuatum cum magnis boteraces, cujus frons extendit ab occidentali pontis Bristolliæ contigue cum longo ponte Bristolliæ, et archus dictæ frontis, [m]*brevis respectû alterius pontis* ad partem orientalem super aquam Avyn.

Turris quadratus pro campanis pulsandis super fundum capellæ predictæ continet in altitudine 18 *(brachia.)*

Capella hospitalis Sanctæ Trinitatis in veteri mercato anglice old market.

Capella Sancti Spiritûs antiquissima juxta ecclesiam Beatæ Mariæ de Radclyff.

Porta prima de Frome-yate ex parte viæ versus ecclesiam Sancti Johannis continet longitudine 20 gressus.

Spacium longitudinis viæ a dicta prima porta edificata, et cum archu, sive longitudo pontis de Frome inter dictas duas portas continet . . gressus.

Porta secunda edificata desuper versus ecclesiam canonicorum quondam Sancti Bartholomei continet in longitudine 12 gressus.

Ecclesia parochialis Sancti Augustini, noviter isto anno 1480 constructa et erecta in longitudine cum duabus alis excepto choro, continet in longitudine 24 virgas.

Latitudo dictæ ecclesiæ, videlicet navis ecclesiæ Sancti Augustini, continet 6 virgas, id est 18 pedes;

[m] "shorter than the other." Butterasses and arches were attached to the old bridge, upon which the chapel was founded.

et quælibet ela continet in latitudine 4 virgas sive 12 pedes ; in toto ejus latitudo continet 42 pedes, mihi relatas per parochianum.

Longitudo cancellæ continebit, quando constructum fuerit, 10 virgas.

Australis pars marisci sexies 60 usque oppositum ecclesiæ Radclyff.

Secunda pars boria ex opposito ecclesiæ de Radclyff usque . . . . . ultra sepcies 60 gressus.

Tercia pars ab extremitate viæ coram . . . . sunt sexies 60 gressus ad portam de Baldwyne-strete. . . .

Incepcio primæ partis de le key Bristoll. incipiendo a porta Baldwyne-strete usque [m]*cornerium capitale incepcionis de le key*, sunt 90 gressus.

Memorandum quod tota longitudo de le key, id est a le graunt corner-place prope incepcionem de le key ex opposito introitus ecclesiæ parochialis Sancti Augustini, sunt quinquies 60 gressus et 46 gressus.

Item a cornerio incipiente transire ad Smalstrete, eundo per templum ecclesiam Sancti Egidii et Sancti Laurencii* ad portam Sancti Johannis, sunt 110 gressus.

Item longitudo ecclesiæ Sancti Joannis cum cripta voltæ continet 50 gressus.

Item a porta Sancti Joannis per Cristmas-strete usque principium portæ et pontis de Frome-yate sunt 124 gressus.

---

[m] " the chief corner entrance into the key.

---

* Now both destroyed.

Et pons de Frome-yate continet 24 gressus.

Item a porta Frome-yate per Lewenysmede usque murum cimiterii Sancti Jacobi, qui est finis ejusdem vici, continet [n]*octies* 60 gressus.

Item vicus vocatus le bak incipit a fine predicti Lewenysmede, eundo de Frome-water ad dictam portam introitus cimiterii Sancti Jacobi, ubi scita est [o]*curta porta*, usque portam de Pyttey-yate, continet 290 gressus.

Et pons ad Pyttey-yate continet 9 virgas.

Item a porta vocata Pyttey-yate usque le pylory ascendendo, vocat. vicus Pyttey, ubi profundus fons scituatur, continet . . gressus.

Item via de le hygh-crosse ad portam Sancti Joannis continet 290 gressus.

Item via de le hygh-cros ad portam Sancti Nicholai continet 200 gressus.

Memorandum latitudo vici vocati Brodemede continet 30 gressus.

Longitudo de le Brodemede continet usque Kyngystrete ad murum [p]*fratrum predicatorum* 300 gressus.

Longitudo chori ecclesiæ fratrum predicatorum continet 26 virgas vel 44 gressus.

Latitudo chori continet 8 virgas vel 14 gressus.

Longitudo navis ecclesiæ continet 31 virgas vel 58 gressus.

Latitudo ejusdem continet 21 virgas vel 34 gressus.

Mauricius Berkley chevalier, dominus castri de Beverstone, obiit 5 die Maii post annum Christi 1466.

[n] "eight times." [o] "a wicket." [p] Dominicans.

Longitudo ecclesiæ navis fratrum Augustini continet 30 virgas vel 54 gressus.

Longitudo chori ecclesiæ *fratrum** Augustini, viz. chorus continet 30 virgas.

Latitudo ejus continet 9 virgas vel 16 gressus.

Longitudo chapter-hous 24 virgæ.

Latitudo ejus 8 virgæ.

Longitudo claustri continet 30 virgas.

Latitudo ejus continet 3 virgas.

1320. Pridie idus Jullii consecratus est locus fratrum heremitarum ordinis Sancti Augustini.

Longitudo navis ecclesiæ fratrum heremitarum Sancti Augustini continet 30 virgas vel 60 gressus.

Latitudo ejus continet 5 virgas.

Est in ecclesia parva navis, et una tantum ala.

In martirologio kalendarii fratrum predicatorum Bristolliæ.

Johannes Vielle armiger, primus vicecomes Bristolliæ, obiit 29 die marcii.

Walterus Frampton obiit die 2 januarii.

Willelmus Curteys, qui fecit fieri magnam crucem in cimiterio, die 2 aprilis.

Ricardus Spicer mercator obiit primo die junii.

Mattheus de Gurnay obiit 28 die augusti, unus fundatorum fratrum predicatorum.

Domina Matilda Denys, quæ obiit die . . octobris anno Christi 1422.

* It is evident that these measurements could not apply to the house of Augustine friars or hermits, but to the Church of the Canons Regular of St. Augustine, now the Cathedral. "Fratrum" was written by mistake for "Sancti." The next article rectifies the error.

Dominus Mauricius de Berkle, et domina Johanna uxor ejus, q jacet in choro in sinistra altaris, die primo octobris.

Dominus Wilelmus Dawbeny miles, qui jacet in choro.

Cor domini Roberti de Gornay jacet in ista ecclesia, qui obiit die 20 novembris.

Dominus Ancelinus de Gurnay, qui jacet in choro, die 15 novembris.

Dominus Mauricius Berkley miles obiit 26 die novembris

1429. Frater Wilelmus Botoner obiit die 15 decembris.

1361. Dedicacio capellæ pontis Bristoll die 4 febr.

Longitudo capellæ 25 virgæ.

Latitudo capellæ 7 virgæ.

Altitudo capellæ 50 gradus, computatur super [q]*quatuor stages.*

Et est volta in inferiori loco pro aldermannis villæ, continet tantam longitudinem sicut ecclesiæ cum navi.

Et 4 fenestræ magnæ quolibet latere, et quælibet fenestra habet 3 luces.

Et alta fenestra in orientali parte altaris continet . .

[r]*Et aliud parvum altare cum parva capella in orientaliori principalis altaris circa longitudinem 3 virgarum.*

Et capella continet voltam, capellam, ac aulam

[q] stages or stories. [r] "And another small altar in a little chapel more eastward of the High Altar."

cum officiis, altam cameram ac altiorem cameram de lapidibus.*

Via Seynt Nicholas strete de porta Sancti Nicholai usque ad principium portæ Sancti Nicholai continet [s]*sexies* 60 et 30 gressus.

Ecclesia Sancti Stephani continet in longitudine 30 virgas.

Latitudo ejus continet 19 virgas.

Altitudo ejus continet 44 pedes; et continet 7 archus in quolibet latere, et continet 7 fenestras; et in quolibet latere et qualibet fenestra 4 [t]*dayes.*

Longitudo partis occidentalis turris Sancti Stephani exterius cum lez boterasses triangulariter continet 9 virgas.

Memorandum quod Kyngystrete a Monkyn-brygge et Erles-medew continet in meridionali parte ecclesiæ cimiterii Sancti Jacobi 1000 gressus.

Longitudo viæ a Monkyn-bryge ex parte occidentali, eundo versus orientem meridionalis cimiterii Sancti Jacobi, dimittendo per Kyngystrete de cruce pontis cimiterii Sancti Jacobi inter angulum [u]*domus pandoxatorii Pownam*, et continuando ad valvam orientalem versus lez barres, ad angulum tenementi patris mei ubi mulieres meretrices manebant vocat. lez barres, continet 200.

---

[s] six times. [t] The space of glass between the mullions. [u] "The house of Pownham, the Brewer."

---

* From this description, it is evident that this Chapel of St. Mary was an elegant Gothic structure. The Chapel on London bridge was likewise so; and that still remaining on the bridge at Beverley is of admirable workmanship.

Et sic continuando viam de Kyngystrete ad pratum vocatum Erlesmedew ad unam altam petram de frestone scitam apud fontem clausum quadratum vocatum Baggewelle . . . .

Via coram aquam Frome, ubi domus elemosinarii scita est, retornando de angulo Brodemede ad principium viæ returnandi de Chedder tenement* ad principium de le slepe ex opposito hostii de le sopemaker continet 50 gressus.

Via returnacionis ad le Pyttey-yate† alias Derych-yate per pontem continet 50 gressus.

Via de Pyttey-yate per le welle usque ad antiquam portam Tourstrete-walle altiori in parte montis de Pyttey continet 130 gressus, intrando viam de Toure-strete versus cimiterium Sancti Johannis Baptistæ coram portam antiquissimam.

Via vocata Seynt Thomas strete usque murum de le toune-walle versus portam de Temple strete seu Radclyff-strete continet 424 gressus a domo sororis meæ, sed a ponte . . . .

Latitudo de Erlesmede de Begghers-well usque aquam de Frome, eundo versus castrum Bristolliæ

* The family of Chedder had large possessions both within and without the town. John de Cheddre was burgess in Parliament in 1298, 26 Edw. I.

"*Inquisit. post mortem Tho. Chedder, Arm.* 21 *Hen.* 6*th.* 1443. Bristol. 84 messuagia, 5 gardin: et 2 claus: et redditus £14. 8s. per ann. Other estates and rent charges in the several Counties of Gloucester 6. Devon 9. Cornwall 2. Somerset 50. Dorset 3." His coheirs were Joan, wife of Richard Stafford, and Isabel, wife of Richard Newton, the Recorder.

† Pithay or Pittey—from the Norman *Puit*, a well, and *Hai* or Hey, a hedge, or inclosure of stone.—Well close.

et le wateryng-place vocat le weer continet 224 gressus.

Longitudo viæ de Erlysmede eundo per Fromewater ad angulum muri castri vocati le were continet 666 gressus in parte meridionali.

In Castel-street alias Seynt Petyr-strete.

Via defensiva Defenstrete* videlicet a Castelstrete veniente de Newyate usque secundam venellam directe intrantem in dictam viam a vico vocato Seynt Petyr-strete coram fonte novo de frestone noviter erecto et fundato de bonis Willelmi Canyngys† ex transverso dictam viam intrantem et defendentem magnum murum inter castrum villæ Bristol. qui quidem murus adherebat *murum defensorem* villæ predictæ.

‡ Dominus Wilelmus Canynges ditissimus et sapientissimus mercator villæ Bristolliæ, decanus ecclesiæ Westbury, obiit 17 die Novembris anno Christi 1474; et exaltatus fuit in ordine presbi-

* Nicholas Excestre, Burgensis et Mercator, by Will 1434. "Item lego Johannæ uxori meæ totam aulam meam cum 14 Shopis, situat' ex opposito placeæ St. Petri, inter shopas Dnæ. Reginæ quas Simon Olyver de novo edeficari fecit ex parte unius venellæ vocatæ Strete-Defence." *Book of Wills. M.S. Archiv. Corporat.*

† By the will of W. Canynge, Jun., 1474, after the demise of his grand children, William and Isabel, a large residuary sum was left to be disposed of by W. Spenser, Mayor, his Executor, who built this conduit, and a hospital for men in Lewin's Mead, opposite to the convent of Franciscans.

‡ Transferred from p. 83 in Nasmith's Edition.

teratûs 7 annis; et quinquies Major dictæ villæ, fuit electus pro republica dictæ villæ.*

Venella prima proxima scituata post introitum de Newgate per viam de Castel-strete alias dictam Seynt Peter strete ex parte boriali, opposita ecclesiæ parochialis Sancti Petri, ubi . . . . . . Olyver juris-peritus [w]*rectidator* Bristoll. manet, continet 60 gressus.

Via vocata Worshyp-strete, aliter vocata Shamells, alias dicta le Bochery, antiquo vocabatur Worshyp-strete, eo quod fuit *vicus honoris* propter mercandisas lanarum veniencium et portum navium oneratarum.

Et sic continuando dictam viam de Kyngstrete a Monkyn-brygge per cimiterium Sancti Jacobi ad angulum Carfox† per tenementa anguli patris mei, eundo continue ad pratum vocatum Erlesmedew ad usque principium dicti prati, ad unam altam petram unius virgæ altam ad Begghers welle scituatam, quæ est ultima libertas franchesiæ villæ

---

[w] recordator.

---

* He was burgess in Parliament in 1451.

† I entertain some doubt as to the meaning of this word. *Carfax* at Oxford evidently means *Quarter-voys, Quadrivium*, and this angle is one of four. *Colfox* is an ancient term for the animal, and it has been likewise either the name of the owner of a corner house, or that it was an hostel or inn having that sign. *Col-Foxe* occurs in Chaucer, and is explained in *Skinner's Etymologicon* to mean a fox of a blackish colour, as coal.

Bristolliæ ex parte orientali, continet in longitudine a dicta via anguli de Barrys 120 gressus; sic via Kyngystret continet a Monken-brygge usque principium Erlesmede 1000 gressus.

Ecclesia fratrum yn Lewelynsmede. [x]

Ecclesia et conventus fratrum Sancti Francisci Bristoll. in parochia Sancti Jacobi in vico Lewenysmede, videlicet chorus ecclesiæ continet in longitudine 28 virgas sive 50 gressus.

Latitudo chori continet 9 virgas sive 18 gressus.

Longitudo navis dictæ ecclesiæ cum duabus magnis alis continet 28 virgas sive 50 gressus.

Latitudo dictæ navis cum duabus alis continet 27 virgas sive 52 gressus.

Latitudo campanilis turris quadratæ continet 4 virgas sive 7 gressus.

Archus 4 sunt in boriali navis ecclesiæ, et tot in meridionali.

Frome-yate.

Longitudo duarum portarum apud Frome-yate continet cum distancia duarum poncium ibi arched ut . . . . flumen de Frome cum naviculis pro bosco oneratis ad manentes super Seynt Jamys bak ac Lewynsmede Brodemede et apud Marchalstret ad fratres predicatores per aquam de Frome possunt cariare boscum mearennium et alia necessaria, continet via de Frome-yate 33 gressus.

Venella brevis et parva prope extra portas de dicta Frome-yate in parte meridionali de Horstrete ex opposita ecclesiæ religionis Sancti Bartholomei ad aquam de Frome continet 20 gressus.

Locus vacuus ad projiciendum sive custodiendum boscum pro igne domiciliorum et alia neces-

x "Leoꝼƿineꞅ-meꝺe."

saria, vocatus anglice a bakk, coram aquam de Frome continet in longitudine 33 gressus.

Latitudo dicti vacui spacii continet circa 20 gressus.

Latitudo portæ Sancti Johannis Baptistæ continet 3 virgas cum duobus pedibus.

Domus de frestone in meridionali ecclesiæ pro conducto aquæ per canales plumbi continet in longitudine . . . .

In vico Sancti Nicholai.

In vico Sancti Nicholai sunt duæ venellæ quarum una transit ad portam orientalem ecclesiæ Sanctæ Werburgæ prope le graunt steyr et continet 120 gressus.

Venella alia in eodem vico Sancti Nicholai prope ibidem in dicta parte alterius venellæ, transit ex opposito directe hostii meridionalis ecclesiæ Sanctæ Werburgæ, 135 gressus.

Ecclesia Sancti Laurencii continet in longitudine 28 virgas.

Latitudo ejus continet 9 virgas.

Latitudo Gylhalde Bristolliæ in vico Bradstrete continet cum capella Sancti Georgii et cellariis 23 virgas.

*Ecclesia Templi.**

Cimiterii amplitudo ex omni parte continet 570 gressus.

Longitudo Templi ecclesiæ continet 53 virgas bis per me mensuratas.

Venella incipiente prope conductum aquæ de Seynt Thomas strete ad Temple-strete continet 100 gressus.

* Holy Rood, Sanctæ Crucis.

Latitudo venellæ continet 3 virgas.

Ecclesia Sancti Thomæ continet in longitudine 43 virgas.

Venella secunda de porta boriali Temple-strete eundo ad Seynt Thomas strete continet 160 gressus.

Latitudo venellæ continet 3 virgas.

Vicus Sancti Thomæ intersecans venellam predictam continet in latitudine 14 gressus.

Venella alia de Seynt Thomas strete adjacens ad Ratclyff-strete, continet longitudo 120 gressus.

Vicus Radclyf-strete continet in latitudine contra dictam venellam 14 gressus.

Venella directe trium venellarum predict de Radclyff-strete in parte boriali ad aquam de Avyn cum le slepe continet 100 gressus.

In parochia Sancti Nicholai.

Venella de vico Sancti Nicholai ad Smal-strete eundo 132 gressus.

Pontis longitudo 184 gressus a principio ad finem anguli viæ le bak.

Longitudo viæ inter duas portas* pontium continet 34 gressus.

Spacium viæ sub qua edificantur duo pontes†

. . . . . .

Muri villæ longitudo a fine key, incipiendo apud lez . . . . viæ de le key, ubi murus

* A gate at either end.

† By "duo pontes" W. W. means the scantlings of timber frame which were thrown out beyond the stone-bridge, and were supported from one pier to another, for the enlargement of the houses. The same was done on the contemporary bridges of London and York.

altus incipit edificii tenementorum abbatis de Bathe, transeundo ad portam Smalstrete, continet 40 gressus; et a dictâ portâ Smalstrete usque portam Sancti Johannis per [y]*altum murum templi* et ecclesiæ Sancti Egidii continet 110 gressus.

Longitudo venellæ viæ vocatæ Myghell-hylle, incipiendo ad ymaginem Sanctæ Mariæ de Horstrete, ducendo ad ecclesiam Sancti Michaelis in occidentali parte de Stepe-strete, [z]*eundo per orientalem ortum fratrum carmelitarum*,† sic continu-

---

y The high wall of the Jews' tabernacle, between St. John's gate and St. Giles' church. z "going by the east side of the garden of the Carmelites."

---

† Now the Red Lodge, and the premises extending to Colston's Hospital. The *Carmelite's* convent and garden were the best and largest in Bristol. Excepting the Gaunts, the three other friaries were mean buildings. Sir John Young, a wealthy merchant, rebuilt the house near St. Augustine's bec; and there received Queen Elizabeth. The Red Lodge was at first a prospect house, belonging to the Prior's garden. The family of Young had obtained the grant of it at the suppression.

It appears that in Broadmead and Lewin's-mead there were many gardens behind the streets. Two of the Mendicant Orders, the Carmelites and Franciscans (White and Grey Friars) possessed large tracts of garden ground near their convents, which were cultivated by their own labour and skill, as they were partly maintained by the sale of their produce. They taught the art of horticulture, then rarely known to, or practised by others. We have in England but few indigenous vegetables: those now so plentifully cultivated have been imported to us, but very few of them before the reign of Henry the Eighth.

ando ad crucem lapideam cum fonte lapidis de frestone continet 170 gressus, versus ecclesiam Sancti Michaelis non multum a cimiterio Sancti Michaelis.

Longitudo venellæ vocatæ Frogstrete prope finem venellæ vocatæ Myghel-hille, incipiendo ad crucem et fontem in alciori parte de Stepstrete, et eundo versus et a retro ecclesiam abbathiæ Sancti Augustini et le Gauntes, continuando ad finem sanctuarii Sancti Augustini, eundo ad locum vocatum Lymotes, continet 840 gressus ad principium montis Sancti Brendani.

Mons Sancti Brandani ecclesiæ ejusdem altitudinis, incipiendo a principio finis de Froglane prope quendam murum in parte dextra, sic eundo per dictum murum, et prope ibidem ascendendo semper usque capellam Sancti Brandani in summitate montis predictæ, continet in altitudine et longitudine viæ circa 840 gressus; et dicitur ab heremitâ custode dictæ capellæ quod altitudo suprema dictæ montis . .*

Capellæ longitudo Sancti Brandani continet 8 virgas cum dimidio.

Latitudo ejus 5 virgas continet.

Circuitus muri capellæ Sancti Brandani continet 180 gressus.

Altitudo montis capellæ Sancti Brandani dicitur, ut heremita ibidem michi retulit, quod nautæ et discreti homines dicunt esse alciorem alicujus pinaculi sive ecclesiæ de Radclyff quam aliarum eccle-

* Brandan Hill rises 250 feet above the lowest level of the present city.

siarum per spacium altitudinis 18 brachiorum (anglice a vathym), et quodlibet brachium continet 6 pedes; et nota quod turris et spera sive pinaculum cum turri quadrata ecclesiæ Beatæ Mariæ de Radclyff continet in altitudine, videlicet turris . . . . pedes et spera pinaculi integri continebat . . . pedes, sic summa tocius altitudinis tam turris quam speræ continet in toto . . . pedes.

Venella tercia super Myghell-hylle citra ecclesiam Sancti Michaelis crucem lapideam et fontem de Stepe-strete videlicet occidentaliorem fontem duarum foncium de petrâ circumgirata.

Ecclesia canonicorum Sancti Augustini.

Dominus Ricardus Newton Craddok miles, justiciarius de communi banco, obiit A. C. 1444, die Sanctæ Luciæ, 13 die Decembris.

Capella Sanctæ Mariæ in longitudine continet 13 virgas.

Latitudo ejus continet 9 virgas et dimidium.

Spacium sive via processionum a retro altaris principalis coram capellam Sanctæ Mariæ continet 5 virgas.

Chori longitudo de le [a]*reredes* principalis altaris usque ad finem chori continet 29 virgas, incipiendo a fine predicti spacii.

Latitudo tam navis chori quam duarum elarum chori continet 24 virgas.

Capella decens* edificata in boriali parte elæ

---

[a] "reredoss."

---

* Bradstone's Chantry.

chori* continet in longitudine . . . . .
virgas.

Via vocata Froglane, cujus principium est in parte boriali ecclesiæ religionum de Gauntes ad finem de le seyntuary, in parte occidentali et boriali dicti sanctuarii Sancti Augustini ordinis, et sic continuando dictam viam per posteriorem viam gardinorum de Gauntes et per murum occidentalem fratrum carmelitarum, sic continuando usque ad crucem et fontem de superiori vico vocato Pylestrete, ex opposito ecclesiæ Sancti Michaelis super montem, ubi tres viæ concurrunt et obviant videlicet via Stepstrete eundo ad Horstrete, alia via in parte occidentali eundo ad Giston-clyff, tercia via eundo ad ecclesiam collegii de Westbery, et alia via versus orientem ad venellam longam Sancti Jacobi . . . .
continet in longitudine 720 gressus.

Via vocata Stanley incipiente ex opposito crucis et fonte [b]*alcioris monticulæ* de Stepe-strete, transeundo usque ad Gyston-clyff per villam de Clyfton continet in longitudine, eundo per montem altissimum capellæ de Brandon-hille dimittendo capellam in dextrâ manu, . . . gressus.

Via vocata Seynt Myghelle-hylle versus ecclesiam [c]*religionum nonitarum* de Sancta Maria Magdalena, ac etiam ad ecclesiam et turrim Sancti

---

[b] "the summit or highest elevation." [c] religiosarum novitarum—"novices."

---

* "Elæ Chori," which affords another proof, if any were wanting, that the Nave of the present Cathedral was the Choir of St. Augustine's.

Michaelis, et similiter ad petram de frestone prope locum justitiæ vocat anglice lez fourches sive galowes, et sic transeundo [d]*cathedralem* ecclesiam de Westbery, continet in longitudine ad montem ecclesiæ Michaelis et ecclesiam religiosarum mulierum Sanctæ Magdalene . . gressus.

[e]*Venella* sive via de le Stipestrete ad crucem et fontem Stype-strete, retornando ad Horstrete ad ymaginem Beatæ Mariæ, continet 120 gressus.

Crux magnifica* apud Hygh-strete, vel vocata Hygh-cros in . . . . continet 2 virgas vel 6 gressus.

Latitudo domus officii justitiæ vocata Gylhalda Bristolliæ continet per viam de Bradstrete 33 gressus sive 23 virgas.

Vicus latitudo de Radclyff-strete incipiente ad pontem Bristolliæ continet in principio dictæ viæ 4 virgas sive 7 gressus; sed ampliat versus ecclesiam de Radclyff ita quod ante venellam proximam in boriali parte ecclesiæ Sancti Thomæ latitudo dictæ viæ continet 12 gressus.

Latitudo venellæ predictæ ex parte boriali ecclesiæ Sancti Thomæ continet 2 virgas.

---

[d] conventualem. [e] "The Lane."

---

* This description of the High Cross is general only; it is "magnifica" only by comparison. William Wyrcestre has never spoken of it more minutely, although it was most perfect in his time, and was remarkable for the excellence of its ornamental architecture, and sculptured regal effigies. The remains of it were removed and re-adapted by Mr. Hoare, and are now placed in the gardens at Stour-head, Wilts.

Turris quadratus ecclesiæ de Radclyff continet in altitudine 148 pedes, et spera . . . .

Maxima campana de Radclyff continet in pondere de lyggeyng wyght septem milia 24 lib.

Secunda campana fere v milia lib. id est IIII milia et . . .

Tercia campana continet MMMCCCLVII lib.

Quarta campana ponderat MMCC lib.

Quinta campana minor continet MDLXX lib.

Sexta minima campana continet MCCC lib.*

Turris Sancti Elphegi continet in altitudine 120 pedes.

Et habet 163 gradus, id est anglice steppys, et quilibet gradus continet 8 pedes [pollices?]

Turris altitudo ecclesiæ de Radclyff continet . .

Speræ altitudo, ut isto die stat quamvis defalcatur ex fortuna procellæ et fulminis, 200 pedes, per relacionem Norton [f]*magistri* ecclesiæ de Radclyff.

Memorandum de le severee duarum fenestrarum unius ex opposito alterius inter duas columpnas continet apud ecclesiam Radclyff 22 pedes, et in longitudine 16 pedes.

Turris et spera sive le broche ecclesiæ carmelitarum de fratribus carmelitarum Bristoll. continet altitudo 200 pedes.

---

f "master mason."

---

* This was a singularly heavy ring of Bells, and such, it is probable, that no other parish church in England possessed. The whole peal has been recast, and enlarged in number. The great Bell at Gloucester is 7000 lbs. weight, less than was that at Redcliff by 24 lbs.

Latitudo dictæ turris continebat nisi 9 pedes ex omni parte.*

Densitudo murorum turris continet nisi duas pedes.

Longitudo duarum portarum de Frome-yate cum spacio longitudinis pontis duarum archuum subtus aquam de Frome fluentium cum spacio intercepto dictarum duarum portarum continet 22 virgas.

Longitudo muri primæ portæ desuper edificatæ continet 8 virgas cum volta lapidibus desuper edificata.

Latitudo secundæ portæ desuper edificatæ continet . . . gressus sive 6 virgas cum domo desuper edificato.

Spatium [g]*interceptum inter duas portas* continet 8 virgas.

Memorandum quod in cimiterio Sancti Jocobi, quasi versus fratres Sancti Francisci, [h]*capella pulcra quadrangula totum de frestone fundata tam in coopertura*† *tecti quam fenestris*, et continet ex

---

[g] "contained within the two gates." [h] "a fair chapel, quadrangular, all composed of freestone, as well in the roofing of the building as in the windows.

---

* Meaning that the internal square of the tower was only nine feet, which must be an erroneous transcript of the MS. Such a diametre could not carry 200 feet, but I know not what number to substitute—perhaps 14, the 9 mistaken for 8, and the decimal omitted. The measurement at p. 58 is 5 gressus, which at 20 inches each, is 8 feet 4 inches.

† This kind of roofing is singular, and very few instances occur to my recollection. There is one still extant in the chancel of Withingham in Cambridgeshire, and another in the Treasury of Merton College, Oxford.

quolibet latere capellæ 18 pedes quadratas cum 8 boterasses.

Capella vocata Knapp* per ipsum fundata pro II presbiteris continet in longitudine 13 virgas, et in latitudine sex virgas.

Latitudo portæ Sancti Nicholai continet 7 virgas.

Via longitudo incipiendo ad pedem pontis Sancti Johannis infra Bradstrete, et continuando per altam crucem de Hygh-strete, eundo directe ad portam Sancti Nicholai per Hygh-strete, continet dicta integra longitudo ad interius partis dictæ portæ Sancti Nicholai undecies 60, quæ faciunt 660 gressus.

Via longitudo ab oriente in occidens, videlicet a loco longitudinis antiquæ portæ villæ citra portam novam vocatam . . . . . ex opposito venellæ in Wynch-strete alias Castell-strete, directe qua itur ad portam sive hostium ecclesiæ Sancti Petri

* The Arms of Knapp are inserted in p. 89.

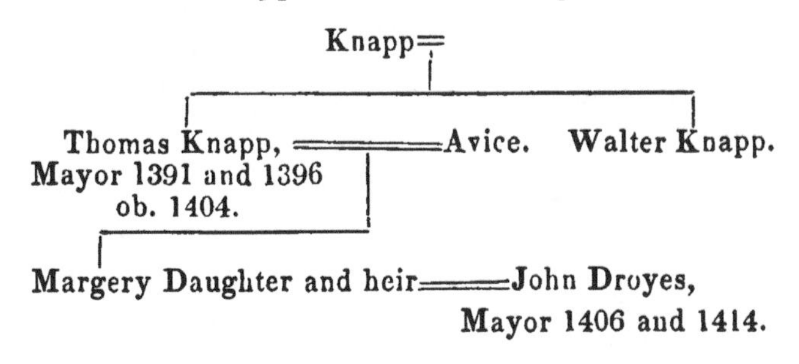

The Chapel on the Welsh Bec, dedicated to St. John Baptist, was founded by Thomas Knapp, for an early Mass to be celebrated by two priests for the sailors leaving the Port of Bristol. He endowed, likewise, two Chantries in the church of St. Nicholas. Vide p. 111.

per domum ubi Ricardus Newton* justiciarius regis manebat quando fuit recordator villæ Bristolliæ, est proxima venella citra Newyate, continet . . . gressus, quæ via est altera medietas tocius integræ viæ ab oriente in occidens.

Ecclesia parochialis Sancti Jacobi prope eccle-

* Newton.

Argent on a cheveron azure 3 garbs or.

Sir Richard Cradoc, firtst called Newton, Recorder, ob. 1444, buried in the Abbey of St. Augustine. Justice of the Common Pleas. = Emma, daughter of Sir Thomas Perrott,

John Newton, of Barrs Court in Bitton = Isabel, daughter and coheir of Richard Cheddre, of Bristol.

Richard Newton = Daughter and heir of Richard Hampton.

John Newton = Margaret, daughter of Sir Anthony Poyntz.

Sir Henry Newton, of East Hartery, Co. of Somerset, ob. 1599. = Catherine, daughter of Sir Thomas Paston, of Norfolk.

In a sepulchral chapel adjoining the South transept of the Cathedral, were brasses, now removed, of Judge Newton, 1444.

A monument, with an effigy of Sir Henry Newton, of Barrs Court, ob. 1599.

Theodore Newton and his son, Sir John Newton, Bart., and Grace his wife, ob. 1661.

siam prioratus in parte orientali villæ Bristoll. continet . .

Ecclesia parochialis prope abbathiam canonicorum regularium Sancti Augustini, in honore Sancti Augustini dedicata.

Ecclesia parochialis in sanctuario Sancti Augustini ex parte boriali villlæ Bristoll. vocata le Gauntes, ubi ecclesia religiosa in honore Sancti Marci dedicata.

Ecclesia parochialis Sancti Philippi in meridionali parte villæ Bristoll. in loco quondam prioratus [i]*religionum* ordinis Sancti Benedicti.

Ecclesia parochialis Sancti Stephani prope le key Bristoll. in loco scituata ubi quondam ab antiquo tempore, ut audivi, fuit ecclesia prioratus religiosorum monachorum ordinis Sancti Benedicti, et fuit cella pertinens monasterio de Glastynbery.

Ecclesia parochialis Sancti Egidii scituata in alto loco ad finem vici de Smalstrete, super portam ad finem viæ dictæ Smalstrete, ad introitum principii de le key [k]*pro navibus applicandis cum mercandisis;* sed dicta ecclesia est unita ad ecclesiam Sancti Laurencii parochialem vel ad ecclesiam parochialem Sancti Leonardi circa tempus regis Edwardi tercii.

Templum judeorum* quondam scituatum sub antiquas voltas directe subtus ecclesiam quondam

---

[i] religiosorum. [k] "for the harbour of ships with merchandise."

---

* Jews' Temple or Synagogue. This room was in a vault beneath St. Giles's Church, where the Jews assembled to worship previously to the reign of King John, who persecuted, and then expelled them.

parochialem Sancti Egidii super principium de le key scituatam, nomine certæ deæ Apollinis vel huic simile honorificatum, ut quam plures gentes michi retulerunt; et modo sunt cellarii pro mercandisis custodiendis in dicto templo prophanato.

Ecclesia parochialis Sancti Laurencii scita directa linea exparte orientali ecclesiæ parochialis Sancti Egidii.

Ecclesia parochialis Sancti Johannis Baptistæ cum volta inferius archuata cum capella Sanctæ Crucis, in qua ecclesia famosus mercator burgensis villae predictæ in tumulo jacet desuper sepultus, et fecit de novo fundari et construi [l]*tam ecclesiam quam portam pulcram cum turri cum alta spera de frestone* cum campanis desuper pulsantibus; et dicta porta est scita contigue ecclesiæ Laurencii ex parte occidentali.

Ecclesia parochialis Beatæ Mariæ vocata Seynt Marye-a-port, et jacet in vico Seynt Mary at Port, directa linea ex parte occidentali ecclesiæ Sancti Petri et turris Bristoll.*

Ecclesia parochialis Sancti Nicholai scita supra portam pulchram vocatam Seynt Colas yate, id est porta Sancti Nicholai, cum turri quadrata et [m]*magnum pinaculum sive spera de mearenno elevato cum plumbo cooperto*, et cum pulcherrima volta de arcu lapidum ac fenestris, cum capella in honore sanctæ crucis.

Ecclesia parochialis Sancti Leonardi scita supra

---

[l] "a church with a fair gate under a tower with a high spire of freestone." [m] a spire of beams of timber framed together *(merennum)*, and covered with lead.

---

* The Keep of the Castle.

portam Sancti Leonardi, cum turri desuper portam pro campanis pulsantibus, sed parva ecclesia, sic scita inter vicum Baldwyne-strete, in quo vico aqua de Frome currebat ab antiquis temporibus ex parte meridionali, ac viam eundo ad keyam et vicum vocatum[n] *Merstrete*, et ad ecclesiam Sancti Stephani ex parte boriali ecclesiæ Sancti Leonardi.

Ecclesia parochialis Sanctæ Werburgæ cum turri condecenti, operate artificiose, pro campanis pulsantibus, scituata in vico principali vocata Corn-strete inter ecclesiam Sancti Leonardi directa linea ex parte orientali et ecclesiam Sancti Audoeni ex parte orientali directe.

Temple-strete; latitudo ejus est 30 gressus in principio . . . . . per totum vicum 22 gressus, 144 gressus.

Venella, via ex opposito ecclesiæ Sancti Thomæ.

Latitudo dictæ viæ continet 10 pedes eundo versus Temple-strete.

Et a fine dictæ venellæ, continuando ad Temple-strete, et retornando versns Stallage-crosse usque ad cornerium vici vocati Toker-strete, retornando ad pontem ex opposito Stallage-crosse in boriali parte de Stallage-crosse versus Touker-strete, continet illa pars viæ de Temple-strete 100 gressus in longitudine.

Via dextræ partis de Toker-strete ultra Stallage-crosse versus magnum fontem ad le slep in angulo finis de Touker-strete, continet 140 gressus a Stallage-crosse.

Via vocata Seynt Thomas strete incipiendo ad pontem usque mansionem sororis meæ in longitu-

[n] Marsh-street.

dine continet, continuando versus muros Bristolliæ par le condyt in Seynt Thomas strete, retornando versus Radclyff chyrch, sic de dicta ponte usque mansionem predictam sororis meæ* continet 160 gressus, et ab inde continuando ad le toune-wall continet longitudo dictæ viæ usque le tonys-wallys 305 gressus.

Latitudo viæ Seynt Thomas strete continet 22 gressus.

Latitudo pontis Bristolliæ continet 9 gressus.†

Via de Hygh-strete, longitudo ejus est ad altam crucem per cokery de Seynt Nicholas yate‡ sunt 176 gressus.

Via vocata Corne-strete ab alta cruce ad portam Sancti Nicholai continet 300 gressus.

Latitudo dictæ viæ ad finem portæ Sancti Leonardi continet 22 gressus.

Via de Mersh-strete ad portam de Mersh-yate continet 360 gressus versus le Mers-yate.

Latitudo ejus continet 9 gressus ad portam de Mersh-yate.

Via quæ incipit a porta de Mersh-yate ad principium de le key, a turri rotunda ubi Burton shyp¶ fuit edificata usque ad mansionem cornerii de lapidibus magnis vocatam Viell-place continet 220

* The wife of John Jay.

† Fifteen feet from one house to its opposite.

‡ Public cooks' shops and taverns. Many of these were placed together in different parts of the town. The lower orders were generally supplied by them.

¶ At that period the largest and most remarkable ship built in Bristol by John Burton, a principal merchant.

gressus; et sic continuando a dicto cornerio domo Henrici Wielle* per longitudinem de le key usque finem ejus erga domum Johannis Pavye† prope templum ecclesiæ Sancti Egidii prope vicum vocatum Smalstrete continet 480 gressus; et sic continet longitudo tocius key coram aquam de Frome 700 gressus.

Via de exteriori parte de Frome-yate vocata Horstrete usque ultiorem domum prope introitum sanctuarii abbathiæ Sancti Augustini, videlicet usque fratres carmelitas ad cornerium in sinistra

* **Vyell.**

Argent a fiss nebulé between 3 annulets, gules.

Henry Vielle=
John Vyell=
1398.
John Vyell=Elizabeth — Henry Vyell=Eliz.

Extract testamento Johannis Vyell Burgensis, Bristol. Dat. 1398. "Item, lego procuratoribus Ecclesiæ Sti. Stephani unum annulum ferentem unum lapidem de Columpnæ ad quam Dominus noster Jesu Christus fuit ligatus; item quod reponatur cum reliquiis in dicta ecclesia."

John Blikker, Burgess of Bristol, dates a deed in 1473, "Et quia sigillum meum est incognitum, sigillum, Johannis Vyell, Junioris, Generosi, apposui."

† William Pavye, Sheriff in 1448, was the father of John Pavye, whose daughter and heir was the wife of Sir John Choke.

manu edificatum coram aquam de Frome continet 360 gressus ; et continuando a dicto cornerio prope fratres carmelitas ad introitum sauctuarii Sancti Augustini continet alias 360 gressus, in toto 720 gressus.

Via de Pyttey a Pyttey-yate, porta vocata Nether Pyttey, usque antiquam portam Pyttey* usque viam ducentem ad Wynch-strete continet 140 gressus.

Pons, longitudo apud Frome de Pyttey-yate continet 10 virgas.

Porta Pyttey-yate continet 4 virgas.

Via a fine Pyttey usque Wynch-street, incipiendo ab angulo de Wynch-strete ex opposito de le pyllorye, continuando ab illo loco ad cimiterium Sancti Johannis ad locum vocatum le blynd-yate, continet 240 gressus, et a dicta porta vocata le blynd-yate usque vicum de Bradstrete per ecclesiam Sancti Johannis Baptistæ continet . . . gressus.

Et dicta via continet in longitudine 140 gressus.

Latitudo dictæ viæ venellæ continet 6 pedes.

Via a porta vocata le blynd-yate veniente de Pyttey-yate per vicum vocatum le Grope-lane, et de Gaste vocatum le Monken brygge continet 180 gressus.

Porta Blynde-yate continet in longitudine et latitudine quadrate 4 virgas.

Via a porta Pyttey usque per Grope-lane usque ad portam vocatam le Blynde-yate supra nomina-

* There were two gates in the Pit-hay, which was anciently inclosed.

tam cum uno retorno continet ut supra 180 gressus usque murum in angulo vocatum le toun-walle.

Via de Pyttey-yate vocata Grope-lane ad viam incidentem usque Blynde-yate continet 120 gressus.

Latitudo viæ predictæ continet 10 pedes.

Via a Monken-brygge usque cimiterium Sancti Jacobi continet 60 gressus ad crucem super pontem coram cimiterium portus Sancti Jacobi.

Latitudo viæ de Bradstrete prope portam Sancti Johannis continet 20 gressus.

Latitudo viæ de Smalstrete ad finem portæ Sancti Egidii continet 15 gressus.

Portæ latitudo nova prope ibidem continet 10 pedes.

Longitudo portæ de edificacione prioris de Bathe continet . . .

Latitudo viæ vocatæ Corn strete ad portam Sancti Nicholai continet 31 gressus.

Latitudo viæ cimiterii Sancti Leonardi est 10 pedes.

Hospitalis domus pro pauperibus in ecclesia quondam canonicorum regularium Sancti Augustini, et modo domus hospitalis pro pauperibus sustinendis in ecclesia Sancti Bertholomei.

Capella decens ab antiquo fundata per se scita, in merdionali parte ecclesiæ de Radclyff, in honore Sancti Spiritus dedicata.

Capella ampla in honore Sancti Georgii fundata par Ricardum Spicer* famosum mercatorem et burgensem dictæ villæ, circa tempus regis Edwardi tercii seu Ricardi regis secundi, et est fraternitas

* Richard Le Spicer, Mayor, 1371.

dignissima mercatorum et marinariorum Bristolliæ dictæ capellæ pertinencia.

Capella in parte meridionali ecclesiæ parochialis Sancti Audoeni, quæ capella est in honore Sancti Johannis Baptistæ, et fraternitas magnifica* pertinet dictæ capellæ.

Capella pulcra scita in amplo cimiterio ecclesiæ parochialis Sancti Jacobi, totum de frestone fundata, et continet 10 pedes longitudinis et 10 pedes latitudinis.

Ecclesia parochialis de kalenders collegii sive fraternitatis vocatæ et fundatæ in honore festi corporis Christi, et ab antiquissimis temporibus fundata ante tempus Willelmi Conquestoris Angliæ circa annum Christi 700, ut per literas certificatorias tempore Sancti Wolstani episcopi sub antiqua manu vidi et legi; quæ ecclesia scita est in meridionali parte ecclesiæ parochialis omnium sanctorum, et ante tempus Edwardi regis tercii fuit scita in ecclesia parochiali sanctæ trinitatis, ut per relacionem . . . . prioris dicti prioratus certificatum fuit.

Voltæ et cellarii 10 in numero, id est 5 voltæ in orientali parte viæ de Bristow-brygge, et 5 aliæ voltæ in occidentali parte de Bristow-brygge cum fortissimis archubus petri clausis et fundatis.

Voltæ duæ in parte orientali viæ eundo ad Bris-

* This gild or fraternity of Merchant Taylors was by far the most wealthy and respectable in Bristol. The term "fraternitas magnifica" in William Wyrcestre's latinity, means only a very rich Brotherhood, in comparison with other Gilds in the town.

tow-brygge, unde una pulcra volta prope portam Sancti Nicholai, unde una est . . .

Volta principalyssima et amplissima, sub capella Beatæ Mariæ fundata.*

Turris rotundus 24 gressus, tunc sunt 100 gressus, et

Turris quadratus 12 gressus, tunc mariscus inter duas turres.

Murus spacium continet 120 gressus.

Turris tercius quadratus continet 9 virgas.

°*Murus vacuus* proxime sequens continet 110 gressus.

Turris quartus quadratus continet 10 virgas.

Murus vacuus sequens continet 94 gressus.

Turris quintus rotundus continet 8 virgas.

Murus vacuus sequitur usque portam Temple-yate continet 100 gressus.

Porta cum turri quadrata, vocata Temple-yate.

Turris alius citra portam Temple-yate latitudinis sex vigarum.

Turris alia ex opposito Seynt Thomas strete latitudinis sex virgarum.

Turris alius inter finem Seynt Thomas strete et portas duas vocatas Radclyff-yates continet 6 virgas latitudinis.

Portæ duæ vocatæ Radclyff-yates desuper edificatæ continet in longitudine . .

Memorandum in mansione pulcherrima de le bak ex posteriore parte de Radclyf-strete super aquam

---

° the wall void of towers.

---

* On the Bridge.

de Avyn est pulcher turris per Willelmum Canyngis edificata,* continet 4 fenestras vocatas Baywyndowes, ornatissimo modo cum cameris, continet circa 20 virgas, in longitudine 16 virgas.

Una porta apud primam portam Mersh-yate per le bakk continet in latitudine muri portarum, in quolibet latere portæ non desuper edificatæ, 2 virgas.

Turres duæ sunt apud le mersh-walle, et quælibet turris continet 16 virgas in rotunditate exterius.

Porta alia in altera parte Mersh-yate, quæ continet 16 virgas in rotunditate, non desuper edificata.

Turris alia incipiente ubi navis Johannis Burton edificata fuit, in circumferentia 16 virgarum.

Turris alia in muro incipiente le graunt key continet ut supra.

Turris prenobilis† per Johannem Vielle armigerum edificata continet in circuitu ultra 30 virgas super primum angulum de le key.

Porta Sancti Johannis Baptistæ.

Turris alius magnus quadratus‡ non multum a

* The house towards the street remains in part, with the Hall and Oratory, the roof of ornamented timber frame still perfect; but this tower with its bay-windows towards the river has not the smallest vestige left. 1833. This must have been a very considerable mansion, as the front extended 60 feet towards the river, and the depth to Redcliff street was 48 feet, according to this account. The ornamented bay-windows were probably in the best style, common in the reign of Henry 6th, of which many specimens may be still seen.

† This Tower was of dimensions to include the whole dwelling-house.

‡ A similar instance.

cimiterio Sancti Joannis . . . . . mercator manet.

Porta prima in altiori loco de Pyttey-yate prope Wynch-strete non super edificata cum domibus.

Turris quadratus [p]*cum mansionibus desuper* pro honesto viro ad murum villæ per 60 gressus ultra Pyttey-yate, vocat Aldrych-yate, super pontem de Frome.

Porta vocata Pyttey-yate supra pontem aquæ de Frome.

Turris rotundus ex opposito Brode mede.

Turris rotundus ex opposito le Seynt Jamys bak.

Turris alius principalissimus quadratus cum multis mansionibus ad pontem vocatum Monkenbrygge, ubi quondam fuit locus fortissimus pro prisonariis custodiendis.

Turris rotundus.

Turris rotundus.

Turris alius quadratus citra Frome-yate edificatus in fine de Cristmasse-strete prope cimiterium Sancti Laurencii, in quo turri honestus vir manet.

Portæ duæ apud Frome-yate fundatæ, et ambo desuper bene edificatæ.

Turris quadratus prope portas Frome-yate directe in angulo finis Cristmas strete, super parvum pontem sive archus coopertus subtus viam anglice vocatam unum slepe, sive gradus circa 30 numero ad aquam de Frome, et una crux de frestone desuper edificata super archum anglice unum vowt.

Turris [q]*longus et largus* quadratus versus turrim

[p] "with chambers built above it." [q] "lofty and large."

de Monken-bryge ex opposito ecclesiæ conventus Sancti Francisci, in quo turri Bagod* manet.

Turris rotundus, non amplus, proximus de turri de le Monken-brygge ex opposito chori.†

The quantite of the dongeon of the castell of Bristol after the information of . . . . porter of the castell.

The tour called the dongeon‡ ys in thykness at fote 25 pedes, and at the ledyng place under the leede cuveryng 9 feet and dimid.

And yn length este and west 60 pedes, and north and south 45 pedes, with IIII toures standyng upon the fowre corners.

And the hyest toure called the mayn, id est myghtyest toure aboue all the IIII towres, ys V fethym hygh abofe all the IIII toures, and the wallys be yn thykness there VI fote.

Item the length of the castelle wythynne the wallys est and west ys 180 virgæ.

Item the brede of the castell from the north to the south wyth the grete gardyn, that ys from the water-yate to the mayng rounde of the castell to the walle northward toward the blak-frerys 100 yerdes.

* Clement Baggod Mayor in 1442.

† It should appear from this description of the Towers, which were connected with the Town walls, that when licence was obtained to repair them, several of the more opulent merchants frequently enlarged them, and made them into dwelling-houses. The most ancient towers were of very coarse architecture.

‡ The largest tower of every Castle is, in modern language, styled "the Keep."

Item a bastyle* lyeth southward beyond the water-gate, conteynyth yn length 60 virgæ.

Item the length from the bullwork at the utter-yate by Seynt Phelippes chyrch yerde conteynyth 60 yerdes large.

Item the yerdys called sparres of the halle ryalle contenyth yn length about 45 fete of hole pece.

Item the brede of every sparre at fore conteynyth 12 onch and viii onch.

Ecclesia hospitalis domus Sanctæ Trinitatis apud Laffordys-yate in mercato.

Ecclesia hospitalis domus Sanctæ Mariæ Magdalenæ leprosorum in occidentali parte de Radclyffe-hylle in boriali parte viæ ad pontem Bryghtbow.†

Hospitalis in ecclesia religionum prioris et conventus Sancti Johannis Baptistæ scitum super aquam Avyn in altera parte ecclesiæ de Radclyff.

Hospitalis domus in ecclesia Sanctæ Katerinæ, ubi magister Henricus Abyndon musicus de capella regis est magister.

Hospitalis domus in vico vocato Lewelynys mede ex opposito ecclesiæ fratrum et conventus Sancti Francisci, fundata per . . . Spencer mercatorem et burgensem villæ de bonis domini Willelmi Canyngys‡ decani collegii Westbery circa annum Christi 1478.

* A Bastyle was a very high embattled wall, not surmounted with towers, as the Bastille at Paris, now erased, was originally built.

† The official seal of this Hospital or Lazar-house of St. Mary Magdalene, at Brightbow, is still extant. It is a very well engraved matrix of bell-metal.

‡ From the contingent bequest of W. Canynges.

Hospitalis domus cum pulcra ecclesia in honore Sancti Laurencii in occidentali parte villæ per dimidium miliare de Laffordys-yate sicut itur Londoniis, pertinenti modo ut dicitur collegio canonicorum ecclesiæ de Westbery.

Ecclesia heremitagii super montem altissimum Sancti Brendani, pertinenti prioratus religionum* Sancti Jacobi, et ut dicitur dictus mons est similis monti Calvariæ prope Jerusalem.

Ecclesia pulcherrima domus templi in honore sanctæ crucis fundatæ in dominio et vico vocato Temple strete, et ei est de magnis libertatibus et frachesiis.

[r]*Heremitagium cum ecclesia in rupe periculossima*† *scita vocata Ghystonclyff, in profundo loco rupis viginti brachiorum profunditatis in dicta rupe super aquam de Avyn, in honore Sancti Vincentii.*

Blake-stonys scita in aqua de Severn apud Holowbakkes, distans a Bristollia ultra Hungrode per 4 miliaria, ubi naves et naviculæ morantur pro

---

[r] "The Hermitage, with an oratory or chapel in the most dangerous part of the rock, called Ghyston Cliffe, situated in a cave of the rock, twenty yards in depth in the said rock, above the River Avon, in honour of St. Vincent."

---

* religiosorum.

† By the expression "*in* rupe periculosissima," it may be concluded that the Hermitage was built within the great cave, as observed of that in the rock of Dover. p. 53.

Nov. 13, 1532. "It'm paied to the Kinge's own hands for his offeringe to o'r Lady in the Rocke, at Dover, iiijs. viijd.—*Henry 8th's Privy purse Expenses*, 8vo. p. 273.

novo refluxu maris, et dictæ rupes parvæ quando mare de Severne incipit refluere versus Bristolliam per Kyngrode et Hungrode et per Ghyston-clyff, ac . . . . cooperiuntur cum mare quam cito, sic per refluxum incepcionis maris omnes naves apud le holow-bakkys de Hispania, Portugallia, Bardegalia, Bayona, Vasconia, Aquitania, Britannia Islandia, Irlandia, Wallia, et ceteris patriis trahunt eorum anchora et disponunt ea velare versus Bristolliam.

Kyngrode . . .

Hungrode in parte altera Ghyston-clyff sed multo inferius versus Kyng-rode in dominio villæ de Lye in comitatu Somersetiæ.

Ecclesia hospitalis Sancti Bartholómei, longitudo ejus continet 18 virgas vel 32 gressus.

Longitudo a pede viæ ducentis ad ecclesiam religionum trium Mariæ Magdalenæ usque ad separationem viæ vocatæ [s]*lez barras* versus Westbery prope ecclesiam Sancti Michaelis, continet 420 gressus, ascendendo ad ecclesiam Sancti Michaelis.

Longitudo ecclesiæ religionum S. Mariæ Magdalenæ continet 27 gressus cum cancella.

Latitudo constat ex navi et tribus elis ac 4 arches.

Longitudo ecclesiæ Sancti Michaelis continet 46 gressus vel 26 virgas.

Latitudo ejus continet 10 virgas 20 gressus.

Turris quadratus campanilæ novæ continet quadrate ex quatuor partibus, quælibet costera continet extra murum 5 virgas.

[s] "The Bars."

Porta borialis ecclesiæ continet XI pedes, et latitudo 10 pedes

Via vocata Grope-lane incipiens ad portam Sancti Johannis Baptistæ, ducens per voltam Sancti Johannis ad prisonam de Monken-brygge ad angulum finis dictæ viæ continet 300 gressus.

Latitudo viæ continet 8 gressus.

Via parva ab Monken-brygge ad venellam venientem et obviantem viam Gropelane ducente ad Blynde-yate continet 100 gressus.

Porta Sancti Johannis continet in longitudine versus Brode-strete 7 virgas.

Longitudo altæ viæ de Hygh-strete de alta cruce usque portam Sancti Nicholai continet 152 gressus.

Johannes Jay secundus maritus Johannæ sororis meæ obiit die 15 mensis Maii anno Christi . . . . filius Roberti Ash, quasi ætatis . . . annorum obiit 19 die septembris, et sepelitur in ecclesia Sancti Thomæ.

1480 die 15 julii, navis . . . . et . . . Jay junioris* ponderis 80 doliorum inceperunt viagium apud portum Bristolliæ de Kyngrode usque ad insulam de Brasylle in occidentali parte Hiberniæ, fulcando maria per . . . .

* John Jay, Senior, was Bailiff in 1456. John Jay, Junior, Sheriff in 1472.

On the floor of the Chancel of Redcliff Church is a slab, inlaid with the portraits of a man and woman in the burgess dress, with smaller, representing six sons and eight daughters.

Hic jacent Johis Jay quondam vicecomes istius villæ, et Johannæ ux. ei. q. qui. quidem Johis Jay obiit .. die .. mens .. A°Dm MCCCC , quoram animabus propitietur Deus, Amen.

et [t]*Thlyde est magister navis scientificus marinarius tocius Angliæ;** et novæ venerunt Bristolliæ die lunæ 18 die septembris, quod dictæ naves velaverunt maria per circa 9 menses, nec invenerunt insulam, sed per-tempestates maris reversi sunt usque portum . . . . . . in Hibernia pro reposicione navis et marinariorum.

Memorandum quod quidem Dynt artifici unius plump-maker villæ Bristolliæ dixit diversis hominibus ab auditu senium et antiquorum gencium, quod retulerunt sibi videre unum arborem vocatum anglice "a haw-tree" crescentem in loco Hyghstrete, ubi crux magnifica scita est.

Item apud viam vocatam le Pylle, eundo inter portam Sancti Lenoardi et introitum cimiterii ecclessiæ Sancti Stephani fuerat domus edificatæ, et pro fundamento fuit ita debile fundamentum quod foderunt 47 pedes [u]*beismurerre* facere fundamentum, et ibi invenerunt in profundo fundamento unam cimbam cum una togh de raycloth, ac etiam invenerunt unam magnam arborem longitudinis 16 pedum squaratum, et demiferunt in fundo nec corruptum sed integre sanum, et . . . .

---

t "Llyde was master of the ship, the most scientific mariner of all England." u Ooze, or slimy mud.

---

* One less skilful would not have been entrusted by Jay, the merchant, upon so hazardous an expedition. He had several successors beside Sebastian Cabot. Robert Thorne, Mayor in 1514, planned a voyage of discovery of a North West Passage, and sailed in 1527, with two of the King's ships, one of which was lost.—*Hackluit's Voyages.*—*Hall's Chronicle.*

Radclyff church.

Dimencio sive proporcio artificiossime de fremasonwork operata in porta hostii occidentalis ecclesiæ Radclyff.*

The west dore fretted yn the hede with grete gentese and small† and fylled wyth entayle‡ wyth a double moolde costely don and wrought.

Latitudo portæ 7 pedes.

Altitudo portæ 9 pedes.

The square yn the dore :

§A champ.
A bowtelle.
A casement.
A fylet.
A double ressant wyth a filet.
A casement.
A fylet.
A bowtelle.
A fylet.
A grete bowtelle.
A fylet.
A bowtelle.
A fylet.
A casement.
A fylet.
A grete bowtelle.
A fylet.
A casement.
A filet.
A lowryng casement.

* Ex informatione Norton, *Magistri Operum* Ecclesiæ de Radclyff. Vide p. 133.

† Carved open work in stone. The term "gentyse" is not found in any architectural glossary which I have seen. "Gentil entaile" occurs in Chaucer's *Romaunt of the Rose*, as applied to goldsmith's work, like lace. May not the term have been transferred to stone?

‡ Entail, "lacework," sometimes used for lace in the poetic description of female dress. I have no doubt but that this term originally confined to *Orfevrie* or goldsmith's work, was adopted by the free-masons for their more delicate and elaborate open-carving in stone. "A worke of rich entayle, and curious molde." *Spenser. F. Q.*

§ See explanation of these terms, p. 102.

A casement.
A fylet.
A bowtelle.
A fylet.
A casement.

A fylet.
A resaunt.
A fylet.
A resaunt lorymer,*
A casement.
A cors wythoute.

Isti 4 proporciones in ambabus:
A champ ashler.†
A cors wyth an arch buttant.‡
A boterasse.
A body boterasse§ and a corner boterasse.

De castro et le dongeon de Bristowe.

Porticus introitus aulæ 10 virgæ longitudinis cum volta archuata de super ad introitum magnæ aulæ.

The inner entre ad porticum aulæ 140 gressus, hoc est intelligere spacium et longitudo inter portam muri de fortificacione murorum de area de le utterward.

Longitudo aulæ 36 virgæ, in gressibus 54 vel 52.

Latitudo aulæ 18 virgæ, vel 26 gressus continet.

Altitudo murorum 14 pedes extra aulam mensuravi.

Aula quondam magnifica in longitudine latitudine, altitudine, est, totum ad ruinam.

Fenestræ in aula duplatæ, altitudo de 11 days continet 14 pedes altitudinis.

* An Ogee, with an edge so deeply carved, as to form a drip or "larmier" to conduct water.

† A water-table of ashler work.

‡ Open or flying arch.

§ A buttress against a plain wall.

Longitudo tignorum aulæ, anglice rafters, continet 32 pedes.

Camera principis, longitudo 17 virgæ, in sinistra parte aulæ regis.

Latitudo ejus cameræ 9 virgæ continet, et per duas columpnas de magnis trabibus paratas* sed valde veteres.

Longitudo de le front coram aula cum . . . 18 virgæ.

Longitudo tabulæ de marble-stone 15 pedes, scita in alia parte aulæ pro mensa regum ibi sedencium.

Turris longitudo in orientali parte turris 36 virgas continet.

Latitudo ejus ex parte occidentali et meridionali 30 virgas continet.

Longitudo de le utter ward castri a media porta, et nuper separata ab interiori warda capellæ principali aulæ camera, continet 160 gressus.

Longitudo primi introitus ad castrum per portum 40 gressus, hoc est intelligendum de vico Castelstrete intrando ad primam portam castri sive vocat. le utterward.

Capella in le utterward, id est prima warda, in honore Sancti Martini est dedicata, tamen in devocione Sancti Johannis Baptistæ, et monachus prioratus Sancti Jacobi omni die deberet [celebrare] in dicta capella, tamen non celebrat nisi per dominicam mercurium et venerem, in septimana.

† The great halls of the more ancient Castles were divided by a row of beams of oak, which were placed upright in the centre to sustain the roof. The old Boothall, at Gloucester, was so constructed, and several others.

Capella alia magnifica pro rege et dominis et dominabus scita in principalissima warda ex parte boriali aulæ, ubi cameræ pulcherrimæ sunt edificatæ, sed discoopertæ nudæ et [w]*vacuæ de planchers et copertura.*

Domus officiariorum coquinæ et hæ pertinentes sunt in interiori warda juxta aulam in parte sinistra, id est in meridionali parte aulæ.

Domus officii constabularii est scita in exteriori warda prima in parte meridionali turris magnificæ,* sed totum ad terram prostratæ et dirutæ [x]*unde magna pietas surgit.*†

Radclyffe.

Hostium occidentale ecclesiæ [Radclyff?] continet 9 virgas‡ et 6 pollices.

Cimiterium ecclesiæ de Radclyff continet 500 gressus.

Crux pulcherrima artificiose operata est in medio dicti cimiterii.

Latitudo capellæ Beatæ Mariæ de Radclyff in occidentali parte ecclesiæ continet 10 virgas.

Longitudo voltæ frettæ archuatæ usque . . .

Altitudo voltæ frettæ archuatæ usque coopertu-ram plumbi . . .

Altitudo voltæ archuatæ tocius ecclesiæ, tam navis ecclesiæ quam duarum alarum, nec non qua-

---

w "void both of floors and roof. x "which is a great pity."

---

* The Keep.

† When Leland saw the Castle it was still farther dilapidated.

‡ pedes.

tuor alarum voltarum et archuatarum, a parte boriali in meridiem continet, computando per numerum graduum 89 anglice steppys, [y]*de terra ad superiorem partem coperturæ tignorum et plumbi cooperancium totam ecclesiam*, secundum relacionem plumbatoris dictæ ecclesiæ mihi dictæ 7 die septembris anno 1480 in dicta ecclesia operante de steppys superius recitatis; et quilibet gradus sive stepp anglice dictus continet 8 pollices ad minus, sic in toto altitudo operis cooperturæ dictæ ecclesiæ continet 53 pedes et 4 pollices.

Longitudo ecclesiæ navis cum choro de Radclyff preter capellam orientalem Beatæ Mariæ continet 113 gressus.

Latitudo [z]*brachiorum* ecclesiæ ante chorum a meridie in boriam continet 67 gressus.

Longitudo capellæ Beatæ Mariæ in orientalissima parte ecclessiæ predictæ continet 16 virgas.

Et omnes boterasse in meridionali parte tocius ecclesiæ cum boterass campanilæ continet 25 in numero præter lez boterasses campanilis quæ continet in numero . . . . boterasses.

Latitudo [a]*trium alarum* in meridionali parte ecclesiæ continet 26 gressus, et 26 gressus in parte boriali ecclesiæ.

In boriali parte ecclesiæ Beatæ Mariæ de Radclyff sunt 16 boterasses, ab orientali capellæ Beatæ Mariæ usque ad principalem capellam sunt 16 boterasses magnæ, quorum aliquæ sunt in latitudine

[y] "From the ground to the highest part of the roof, of timber frame and lead, which covers the whole church."

[z] The Transept.

[a] three aisles.

inferius apud le table versus et prope terram 2 virgarum, et aliquæ boterasses minus.

Quantitas [b]*rotunditatis principalis* capellæ Sanctæ Mariæ [c]*cum ymaginibus regum operatis subtiliter in opere de frestone* continet in circuitu, cum hostio introitus subtiliter operato 44 virgas.

In via de Radclyff in parte . . . . . . sunt . . . venellæ.

Prima venella est prope murum de le toune-wall vocata . . . .

Longitudo trium alarum in parte boriali ecclesiæ de Radclyff continet 15 virgas, et tot virgæ latitudo in parte boriali ecclesiæ.

Secunda venella sequens est Howndon-lane et continet . . . . gressus.

Tercia venella est in meridionali parte ecclesiæ Sancti Thomæ et continet . . . gressus.

Quarta venella in meridionali parte ecclesiæ Sancti Thomæ prope ibidem ecclesiam continet . . gressus.

Quinta venella est ex altera parte cimiterii Sancti Thomæ, ubi tumba David Ruddok* est facta in quodam muro, et continet 180 gressus.

In alia parte viæ de Radclyff-strete proxima aquæ de Avyn, in boriali parte viæ de Radclyff, est prima venella a porta de Radclyff-yate, usque aquam Avyn, et continet 150 gressus, ubi dominus Moysi Lombardus manebat . . . . .

Portæ duæ in fine de Radclyff-strete cum spacio

---

[b] "circular space." [c] "with statues of Kings, curiously wrought in free-stone."

---

* Sheriff, 1419.

de le wateryng-place ac conducto parvo in le wateryng-place continet 32 gressus, sed spacium inter duas portas continet 20 gressus.

Memorandum quod venella in parte boriali de Radclyff-strete transiens usque Avyn-water.

Venella secunda alia versus pontem Bristolliæ non multum distat a prima venella, quasi [per] spacium 60 gressuum, et continet in longitudine circa 110 gressus.

Venella tercia in eadem forma coram aquam de Avyn, transiens cum unâ viâ ad aquam de Avyn anglice a slepe, aliter . . . . . et continet in longitudine ad aquam de Avyn* . . . . . et est ex opposito venellæ in altera parte venellæ eundo ad ecclesiam Sancti Thomæ.

Longitudo viæ in parte occidentali ecclesiæ religionum et hospitalitatis Sancti Johannis Baptistæ ex altera parte turris ecclesiæ de Radclyff continet 154 gressus usque aquam Avonæ.

Latitudo dictæ viæ continet 3 virgas.

Heremitagium est scitum in occidentali parte ecclesiæ Sancti Johannis super aquam Avonæ, in rubeo clivo super aquam Avonæ anglice Avyn.†

Longitudo viæ in parte boriali super Radclyf-hill, ultra ecclesiam de Radclyff in parte dextra versus calcetum de Brightbow, et citra domum hospitalis Beatæ Mariæ Magdalenæ, conducens ad molendina super aquam Avyn scita de lapidibus murata, continet 400 gressus, et vocatur ‡. . . myllys.

* a repetition.

† Hermitage of St. John on the opposite Bank of Redcliff.

‡ Trene.

Latitudo viæ molendinorum continet 3 virgas.

Ecclesia hospitalis Sancti Johannis Baptistæ ex opposito ecclesiæ Beatæ Mariæ de Radclyff.

Longitudo aulæ continet 21 gressus.

Latitudo aulæ continet 13 gressus.

Longitudo claustri continet 32 gressus.

Latitudo claustri continet 30 gressus.

Stagnum aquæ conductus quadratus est in medio claustri.

Porta ad venellam sive viam in parte occidentali ecclesiæ quam prope murum ecclesiæ predictæ usque ad aquam de Frome continet 150 gressus.

Latitudo portæ et viæ 4 virgæ.

Longitudo ecclesiæ Sancti Thomæ continet 73 gressus sive 48 virgæ.

Latitudo ejus continet 21 virgas.

Latitudo portæ Sancti Nicholai 4 virgæ: longitudo portæ 9 virgæ 14 gressus.*

Latitudo portæ Sancti Leonardi 4 virgæ: longitudo portæ 9 virgæ in parte orientali.

Latitudo portæ Sancti Johannis 4 virgæ: longitudo portæ 7 virgæ.

Latitudo portæ Newgate 4 virgæ: longitudo dictæ portæ 9 virgæ.

Latitudo viæ Sancti Thomæ incipientis apud pontem Bristolliæ 4 virgæ.

Jovis ultimo die augusti applicui Bristoll.

Dominica 10 die septembris equitavi ad colle-

* Near St. Nicholas gate was an establishment of Cooks' shops. Walter Frampton, by will in 1388, leaves a tenement in "Coking-rew." Others were in the passage behind All Saints Church.

gium Westbery, et locutus fui cum Johanne Gryffyth de Bristoll. merchant ibi morante.

Item equitavi usque Shyrehampton, loquendo cum Thoma Yong armigero, pro 11 libris meis recuperandum, unum de libro magno ethicorum, alium de libro vocato le myrrour de dames* cooperto rubeo coreo, et [d]*jantavi* secum, dedit michi letum vultum pro amore patris sui, cum uxore ejus sui favore.

Dominica predicta applicui Bristoll.

Martis 12 septembris fui apud Ghyston-clyff et mensuravi rupem profundum usque heremitagium ad profunditatem 20 brachiorum, et unus juvenis officii fabri dixit mensuram residui rupis dicta die michi ad aquam anglice ebbyng-water, et dixit mensurare a capella dicti heremitagii 44 brachia, sic in toto continet 64 brachia profunditatis.†

Martis 26 die Septembris, fui apud heremitagium ultra aquam de Avyn, quando mare exiit id est ebbyng-water, per villam Rownam in batilla conductus, directe in monte opposita seu contraria Ghyston-clyff in dominio Ashton, cujus dominus est Johannes Chok‡ chevalier.

---

d "breakfasted."

---

* Translated into French by Lawrence Premierfaict.

† In English, p. 54.

‡ There is a Tomb erected for Sir Richard Choke in Ashton Church. The arms are upon the Tomb, and in the window above it.

"The howse of the Choks was first greatly avaunsed by Choke, Chefe Juge of England, that attayned lands to the some of 600 marks by the yere, and kepte his chefe house at Longe Aschton, by Bristow, having great furniture of sylvar." *Leland. Itinerary, v. 7. p. 84.*

Memorandum quod isto anno Christi, 1465, die epiphaniæ Bristoll, relatum fuit mihi per Elizabet Nicholl, quod Elizabet Nicholle, [e]*commater mea* obiit per 35 annos preteritos, viz. quando Leycestre fuit major London.

---

[e] "my Godmother."

Chocke.

Argent, three cinquefoils pierced, gules.

Pedigree of Choke, of Long Ashton.

G. 19, Visit. Somerset, Cooke.

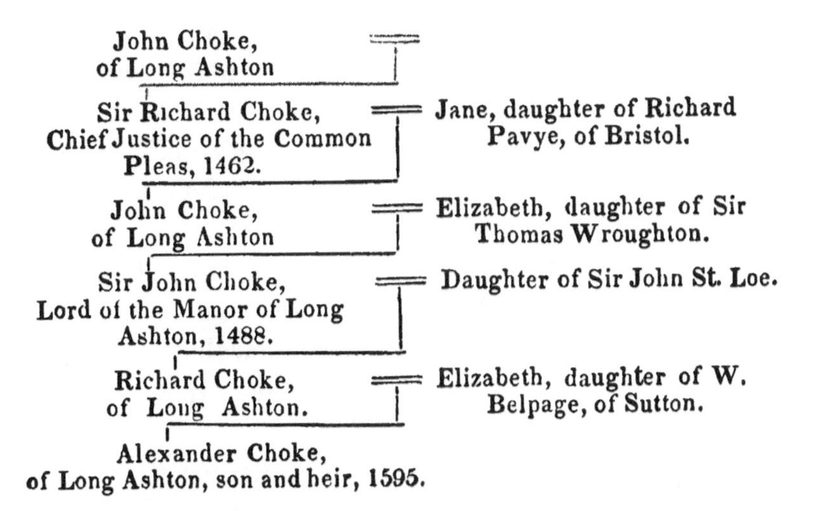

Et dicto anno. scilicet in anno. Christi 14 . . viz. die commemoracionis animarum, Willelmus Nicholl et . . . . . maritus [f]*Elizabet* consortis suæ velaverunt in duobus navibus, unus in navi Phish vocata le Cog-Anne,* et alter vir maritus Elizabet in navi Thomæ Erle, extra le kyngrode, et ambo perierunt in vigilia Sanctæ Katerinæ proxima post, [g]*cogita* de die transitus ejus, viz. le Cog-Anne submersus, et alius navis captus per Hispanos.

Memorandum quod die Sanctæ Trinitatis proxima ante captionem dictarum navium, Elizabet Nicholl filia Isabellæ Nicholle erat sponsata cuidam mercatori.

Memorandum quod die Sanctæ Margaretæ anno Christi, 1402, Matilda Botoner [h]*avia mea* obiit, et executores ejus fuerunt Thomas Botoner filius ejus

---

[f] "Elizabethæ." [g] "The Cog." [h] "my Grandmother."

---

* The term "*Cog*," as applied to a particular kind of vessel, is of very early application. *Matthew Paris* has "Cogones." 1066. venit Gul' Conq. in Angliam cum 300 cogonibus. *Spellman*, in his Glossary quotes *Chaucer*:—

> "He found Jason and Eracles also
> Shutte in a Cog to land were y go."

In the more ancient poem of *Richard Cæur de Lion*, different vessels are particularised—

> "Cogges and Dromounds, many galeye,
> Berges, Schontes, Trayeres felè,
> That were charged with al wele,"

to accompany that heroic king in his expedition to the Holy Land.

A barge or lighter was called a "Balenger."

et Willelmus Wyrcestre [i]*filiaster ejus*, et habuit exitus dictum Wilelmum Botoner, Elizabet sponsatam Willelmo Wyrcetyr, et Aliciam sponsatam Thomæ Benysham.

Memorandum quod mense Julliï, anno quinto regis Henrici quinti Willelmus Wyrcetyr primo inhabitavit in tenemento Colyns in Bermodsey-strete.

Anno 48 regis Edwardi tercii, tenementum patris mei in Brodemede fuit venditum Thomæ Botoner [k]*avo meo* et T. Botoner filio suo primo genito.

Anno secundo regis Henrici quarti, W. Wyrcestre pater meus primo cepit in firmam tenementum Johannis Sutton super le bak in parochia Sancti Jacobi, in quo tenemento W. Wyrcetre natus fuit.*

Anno Christi 1412, Johannes Randolf obiit, et fecit executores, Agnetam consortem suam et Willelmum Knolyn.

Memorandum quod Adam Botoner de Coventre fuit frater Thomæ Botoner avi mei, per relacionem Agnetæ Randolf [l]*amiciæ meæ* et . . . . Bracey filiæ ejus; et dictus Adam [m]*habuit exitum* Agnetam Botoner de Laffordes-yate Bristolliæ, et obiit apud Coventre tempore magnæ pestilenciæ,

---

[i] "her Son-in-law." [k] "my Grandfather." [l] "my Aunt."
[m] "had issue."

---

* *Deed dated* 41 *Edw.* 3 *tij.* 1368. Walter Staunton, Burgensis, &c. confirmasse dedisse and concessisse *W. Wyrcestre, Glover*, totum illud tenementum quod nunc inhabitat, quod extendit se a vico (St. James's Bec) anterius usque ad aquam Froome posterius, &c.

anno Christi 1386, et misit filiam suam prefatam Bristolliæ ad Thomam Botoner fratrem suum custodiendam, et quidam Johannes Randolf de Laffordes-yate duxit dictam Agnetam de Coventre ad Bristoll.

Memorandum de nominibus Tychemersh prope villam Wyrcestre, vel prope villam de Ekyngton prope Pershore, quod ipsi sunt de consanguinitate Willelmi Botoner et Agnetæ Randolf secundum suam relacionem.

"A maner latin corrupt, was his speche,
But algate therby was he understonde."

CHAUCER. *Man of Lawes tale.*

FINIS.

AN ESSAY

ON THE

Life and Times of Wm. Canynges,

MERCHANT, OF BRISTOW,

Robert Canynges, of Touker's street, in Bristol, 1322 =

2. Robert Canynges, 1340.

1. William Canynges, of Touker-street, Mayor in 1372, 1373, 1375, 1381, 1385, 1389. Will dated 1396. = Agnes, daughter of John Stokes, whose tomb is in the Church of St. Thomas, as mentioned in the will of William Canynges.

2. Simon Canynges. = Margaret. Will dated 1414.

Thomas Canynges.

1. Joan = John Milton. Mayor 1433.

1. John Canynges. Mayor 1392, 1398 = Joan, daughter of John Wootton.

Thomas Young, of Redclive-street. Mayor 1420.

John Burton, of Redclive-street. Will dated 1454 = Isabel

1. Agnes.
2. Julian.
3. Margaret.
All these children were left under guardianship in their father's will.

1. John Canynges, ob. inf.

2. Thomas Canynges, Lord Mayor of London in 1456. Ancestor of the Canynges, of Foxcote Co. Warwick, and of Baron Garvagh, of the Kingdom of Ireland, and of George Canning, whose widow was created Baroness Canning, 1828.

3. William Canynges, the restorer of St. Mary Redclive Church. Mayor in 1441, 1449, 1456, 1460, 1466. Will dated 12th Nov., 1474, ob. 1475. = Joan, daughter of —— buried in Redcliffe Church, 1466.

Alice Young, ux. Thomas Pyncheon.

Thomas Young, Recorder. Justice of the King's Bench. = Isabel Burton, daughter and sole heir.

Thomas Young, ob. 1500, buried in Redcliff Church.

1. William Canynges, ob. vitâ patris, 14 . . . = Isabel or Elizabeth, daughter and heir of William Vowell, of Wells, remarried to John Depedene, Esq., marriage settlement, dated 1457.

2. John Canynges, ob. vitâ patris. = Elizabeth, daughter of —— mentioned as a widow in the will of William Canynges.

1. Thomas Canynges, heir of his mother's jointure in Bristol and Wells; of age before 1484, when he sold Canynges-Place in Redcliff-Street, after a law suit with W. Spenser, his Grandfather's executor, which was determined in his favour.

2. William. ob. inf.

1. Isabel, ob., inf.

Both endowed in their grandfather's will, with remainder for other purposes.

ESSAY ON

William Canynges,

(Read at the BRISTOL INSTITUTION, in April, 1831.)

Biography belongs to the peculiar country of the individual whose life is narrated; or to the local situation in which it has been beneficially passed, and to these circumstances it owes its chief interest. Public services command the most lasting fame, but private worth the most grateful memory. But how is a private man to be remembered at all after a lapse of four centuries, since he existed? No satisfactory memorials can now be found, but in some munificent establishment of charity or sumptuous and beautiful buildings, and of the "man as he was," we can glean, at so distant an interval of time, no intelligence, excepting from documentary evidence. Such has been afforded in an authentic, although, of course, in a limited degree. We must acknowledge the penury of private history, in which so little can be distinctly seen, through the veil of time or the mist of panegyric. This will be the simple record of a private life. Of William Canyngesand his family, as among the superior merchants of Bristol, considerable facts may be collected from their wills (copies of which are preserved in the archives of the Corporation), and numerous deeds* and transfers of property now in the possession of Mr. Cumberland, who has obligingly allowed them to be consulted, for the purposes of this Essay. From these, extracts will be made to corroborate various assertions, with respect to their large possessions within the limits of this ancient town and its immediate environs. A confusion in the first pedigree given of Canynges, may be thus corrected; as far as the mistaking the individuals, of dates and their respective position, which I have been enabled to authenticate, by these means.

Although the genealogy of this estimable man will, by a diligent investigation, be placed in a clearer point of view than has been hitherto done, his were the simple transactions of private life, which will find an interest with those only who care about our own local history. I must therefore excurse not a little, and endeavour to make frequent digressions not uninteresting accessories to my present attempt of offering a panoramic view of his times, and this will be best effected by adverting to the state of maritime discovery, and

* A large collection was likewise in the possession of the late Reverend S. Seyer, the Historian of Bristol, who presented them to the City Library.

the principles of commerce as then practised, the habits and domestic manners of his contemporary merchants, and more than all, the perfection of church architecture, to which he so magnificently contributed.

These are the general outlines of this essay. Fully aware that antiquarian researches, when pursued with minuteness, are considered by many is dry and unimportant, yet, as in the establishment of truth, the advancing proofs of undeniable facts is much more to be valued than the most ingenious conjectures, I shall hazard the imputation of tediousness, which they may occasion.

Of the family of William Canynges, previously to their settlement in Bristol, nothing can be related with certainty; and more than sufficient latitude of conjecture might be required to connect them with others of the same name. The industry of the genealogical antiquary must not pretend to command more than a peculiar interest, or that in which individuals are concerned.

Two ecclesiastics rose to eminence. Simon de Canynges was the 24th Abbot of Hyde, near Winchester, in 1292; and John de Canynges, the thirty-fifth Abbot of Abingdon, in 1322.* A village is called Bishop's-Canynges in Wiltshire, where a family of the same denomination appear to have resided in the 14th and successive centuries, several of whom were tenants of the manor of Minety, not far distant, under the Abbot of Cirencester,†

* Willis. Mitred Abbeys.

† Inquisitio post mortem 9 Edw. 3tij; 46 Edw. 3tij.

about the period, when we have the earliest evidence of them, as "burgesses of Bristow." In the municipal rolls of Mayors and Bailiffs, the name of Canynges does not occur before the year 1369, when William Canynges was in so high an estimation, both as to wealth and probity, that he was elected as chief magistrate for no less than six times, between the years 1372 and 1389. He was likewise their representative in parliament. His will, preserved in the city archives, bears date in 1396.* He bequeathes houses and premises of extent and value in Touker-street, and desires to be buried in our lady's chapel in the church of St. Thomas. John his son, who was likewise Mayor in 1391, ordains his sepulture in the same place;† and Simon, another son mentioned in that will, was, in pursuance of his own will, buried in the church of St. Stephen.

From their establishment in Touker-street, it is evident that they were first occupied in the manufacture of cloth, as confined to druggets and blankets; for it is known, that all cloth of a finer texture and quality was then imported to us, either from France or the Low Countries. The Toukers or Clothiers (so called from the great manufactories on the river Toque, near Abbeville, in Normandy) are said to have been first brought to this country under the patronage of the Knights Templars, in whose church here, they established their chief

* Wills. Corporation Archives. Barrett's list.—Hist. of Bristol.

† Will dated May 13, 1405.

gild or fraternity, which remained as one of the more considerable, to the time of the dissolution; and their chapel is still extant. They had obtained from the Templars a grant of a very extensive field near the river, called in old surveys "the 'Rack hythe,' in which the tenters for stretching and drying cloth were erected. They had likewise the treen or wooden mills for fulling, below Redcliff, near Bedminster. In fact, during the long reign of Edward the Third, and that of his successor, the geatest encouragement was held out; and the division of the town beyond the Avon was principally inhabited and occupied by such manufacturers, in its several branches. It is curious to observe, how minutely these are discriminated in the several wills, in Mr. Cumberland's collection of that date, as Fullo, Clothier—Textor, Weaver—Tinctor, Dyer, &c.; the general name for a clothier was "a webbe," which Chaucer has introduced as a personage in his Canterbury Tales; and in 1351, we have the will of Peter Herte "Webbe."*

This digression is, perhaps, necessary to an accurate statement of the exact position in which the Canynges were placed, when they were at first ranked among the more eminent burgesses of the town, and as it points out the source of their great subsequent wealth before they became merchants, and exported the cloth of their own manufacture.

In the wills of both William and John Canynges, a small tenement only in the parish of St. Mary Redcliff is recited. From this circumstance, a

* Proved by several Wills. See p. 80.

doubt suggests itself, whether the first William Canynges were actually the first rebuilder of Redcliff church, as he was not an inhabitant of the parish, but of that of St. Thomas, where his estate lay, and where both himself and his son had directed their sepulture. The fact in question rests, at present, upon a tradition only, unconfirmed by any evidence, that has hitherto been brought to light, and which will, in due course of this inquiry, lead me into farther discussion.

William Canynges (for thus, in every document I have seen, he designates himself), the grandson of the first noticed, was born in Bristow, in the year 1400, as far as can be ascertained by the statement of his age, at the time of his decease, November 12th, 1474. His will was proved Sept. 26, 1475.

He was the third son of John, son of the first mentioned William, and that fact is authenticated by the pedigree, which accompanies this memoir, for the satisfaction of the genealogical inquirer. His father died in 1405, and as it appears, made his will during his last sickness, for it bears date in the same year. He largely portions his wife, and identifies six children, to whom he bequeaths legacies and remainders. Thomas and William were his surviving sons, but of his daughters nothing is known with certainty. Of John, the first mentioned in the will, it may be presumed that he died an infant. Thomas, the second son, was established in London, where he attained to great wealth and civic honours. He was enrolled in the Grocer's company, and was probably a merchant, trading to the Levant. In 1450 he was Sheriff, and in 1456 Lord Mayor of London.* From him descend a very respectable family of the Roman Catholic persuasion, which have held the manor of Foxcote, in Warwickshire, for more than three centuries. The late George Canning, who had reached to so high a degree of political superiority, had a legitimate claim of lineal alliance to that branch. After the death of John Canynges, Joan, his widow, remarried with Thomas Young, a merchant of the first rank, and an inhabitant of the parish of St. Mary Redcliff, by whom she had Thomas Young, who was bred to the law, and subsequently advanced to be one of the Puisne Justices of the King's Bench, in 1476.

William, the subject of our present investigation, was only five years old, at the early death of his father, but the fostering care of his mother's second husband, amply supplied that loss. His genius and education were directed by him to mercantile pursuits; and he had experience of whatever might insure to him the good fortune of his future life, in the opportunities of learning the modes of commerce, in one of the most extensive and opulent establishments, in Bristol, subsisting at that period. That he soon discovered most valuable talents in such pursuits, can not be doubted. The effects in such regular movements usually follow the cause; and there was an early promise of his great success.

No document ascertains his progress before the

* *Stowe's* Survey of London, and MSS. Coll. Arm.

years 1432 when he was Bailiff, 1438 Sheriff, and 1441 when he was elected Mayor. Few anecdotes concerning him have descended to posterity; and nearer to our own times, a great difficulty presents itself in tracing the simple transactions of the private life of those, who are known to fame. It will be allowed, that William Canynges had the singularly good fortune to have concentrated all the commercial habits of his predecessors, and the merit of improving them.

All that can be advanced with certainty must be from irrefragable documents, as far as he was concerned with his fellow burgesses, as their municipal magistrate, and their representative in parliament.

The first noticed honour he enjoyed five times; one less than his grandfather had done. These facts admit of a certain explanation. During the lapse of several centuries before the reign of Charles the first, the fee farm of the Town and Port had been always held, in lease, by burgesses; and the Mayor was officially the Seneschal of the King. The castle was then a royal demesne with a distinct jurisdiction. This circumstance made it absolutely expedient in turbulent or warlike times, that the Mayor should be connected with the existing government, because levies both of ships and money were frequently recurring, the writs for which were directed to be executed by him; and the royal influence was exerted to continue the same officer, longer than the ancient constitution of the Burgh, would seem to warrant. He was first returned to parliament in 1451, and subsequently in 1455.

Highly as this distinction is now valued, it was then considered as an *onus*, not only by the borough, but by the individual elected, in those simple times. The representatives of Bristol had daily wages, and an allowance given for their journeys.

Canynges having arrived at his fortieth year, there is satisfactory evidence, that he had exceeded his contemporary merchants in influence and wealth. Chaucer, in his prologue to the Canterbury Pilgrimage, had preconceived his exact portrait :—

> "This worthy man ful wel his wit besette;
> Ther wiste no wight that he was in dette,
> So stedefastly didde he his governance,
> With his bargeines, and with his chevisaunce.
> —Forsothe he was a worthy man withalle." *

The word "chevisaunce" means any contract for money.

And here we must pause, to take a general view of the causes of this extraordinary opulence; of the nature and conduct of the trade of England as carried on with other European nations; and lastly of the principal merchants then resident in Bristol, who lived and thrived with him, and who traded from the same port, with comparative success. If such an investigation should be satisfactory, we shall agree with the honest narrator William of Wyrcestre, that he was "ditissimus et

* In modern English.—"This worthy man applied his talents beneficially, so that no man could say that he was indebted to him, so honourably did he conduct his mercantile affairs, in all his bargains and transactions of money."

sapientissimus mercator,"* and that this was the meed and the effect of his singular prudence, and of his sagacity in mercantile adventure. But previously to confining the present inquiry to these individuals, a concise sketch of the state of navigation and commerce, as they subsisted between this, and other European nations, in the fourteenth and fifteenth centuries, may not be considered as irrelevant. The chief commodity, and the most valuable medium of commercial intercourse, was wool. Our numerous flocks fed on downs of scarcely measureable extent, supplied an abundance equalled by the superior quality; and which was very partially manufactured in England, before the period now mentioned. It was sent to Flanders and the north of France, where were manufactories of fine cloth, which was exported into England.

King Edward the 3d has been justly designated, by all the writers on the subject, as the father of English commerce. The impost upon wool formed a great part of his revenue, and, as it was received in kind, by the chief landed proprietors from their tenants, as by him, it had gained the value and currency of money. For these receipts he established the ten staple towns, of which Bristol was one; and the official seal is still preserved among the city archives. About the middle of his reign, he endeavoured to transfer the making of fine cloth to England, and for that purpose had invited several Flemish clothiers to settle here. We have the evidence of Flemish and French names as

* William Wyrcestre, p. 83.

Fraunceys, Beaupigne, Blanket,* and others, to prove that some of them were established in Bristol. Blanchett or Blanket was the first who obtained a licence for setting up looms in his house; and he there manufactured the kind of cloth, which is in general domestic use, under that name. Worsted had its denomination likewise from a town in Norfolk, whither the Flemings had brought the art of making it.

The far greater number of the statutes of Edward 3d were passed to protect and encourage navigation and commerce, by prohibitions which were not always beneficial in their results. Trade was opened to the Baltic, to Denmark, Iceland, and the North Seas. There was a considerable traffic to Normandy, Flanders, and Spain for wines, but the Mediterranean, at this period, was only partially navigated by English vessels, on account of the frequent piracies to which they were exposed from the active jealousy of the Italian merchants.† Notwithstanding, reprisals were made, and several Genoese were resident in Bristol, as Giovanni Gaboto, the father of the discoverer of Newfoundland, whom we recognise as Sebastian Cabot,‡ and

* These names occur in many deeds and wills of that date, as well as in the roll of Civil officers.

† Anderson's Hist. of Commerce v. i. p. 375. Macpherson's Annals of Commerce, and Campbell's Political Survey.

‡ Sebastian Cabot (Gaboto). "His history has been enveloped in obscurity. What has been most commonly alleged respecting him is false; and numerous writers, in speaking of the voyages which they did not doubt he performed, have made them a ground work of misconception, pretension and falsehood. Now since the labours of Sebas-

who was a native, of no common celebrity. About that time the ships of Pisa, Genoa and Venice had arrived in many of the English ports, and Bristol had its full share of that intercourse. They imported silk, spices, and other produce of Italy and the Levant. Still the Italians strenuously opposed the admission of English vessels into their ports, but having

tian Cabot are the starting point of English discovery, the obscurity and the ignorance prevailing on the subject, have involved the subsequent stages of his history, in error and confusion. He was an Englishman, and sailed from the port of Bristol, in search of a Northwest passage; was the first discoverer of North America, and touched upon the *terra firma* of the Western world, even before the great Columbus, and though others have the fame of it, was the first commander who ever steered his bark into the Straits which have been since named after Hudson. These are remarkable truths, but not more remarkable than the vulgar errours, which vanish in the demonstration of them. The Venetians claim him as their countryman. But the most authentic evidence is that given by Richard Eden, the author of a very scarce and valuable repertory of voyages and travels entitled "Decades of the New World," as it was derived from Cabot himself. Eden asserts—"Sebastian Cabot tould me that he was born in Brystow, and that at iiij yeare olde he was carried with his father to Venice, and soe returned againe into England, with his father, after certain yeares, whereby he was thought to have been borne in Venice." See "*A Memoir of Sebastian Cabot, with a review of the history of Maritime Discovery.*" *8vo.* 1831.

The point thus established, is, that Cabot was not only an inhabitant, but a native of Bristol. His portrait, when an old man, was painted by Holbein, and in the possession of C. J. Harford, Esq. It is engraved in Seyer's Memoirs.

discharged their cargoes here, they took back stock fish and wool. Frequent conflicts took place between the mariners of the two countries, and the damage done, was upon application to the government, always levied upon the Italian merchants, especially Genoese, who were settled in any of the ports to which the pirated ship belonged, and whose grand object was the exclusion of all others from the Mediterranean, and the monopoly of the stores of the East. Fabyan, in his chronicle, mentions such a spoliation of a large vessel, belonging to Robert Sturmye, a merchant of Bristol, for which, the Genoese merchants of London were fined and committed to the Flete prison.*

The various obstacles which originated in these several causes—the barbarous state of society and manners, national antipathies—or fraudulent and arbitrary measures of governments and princes, did not prevent the merchants of our own, as well as different countries, from acquiring an excessive opulence, which equalled the rentals of the ancient nobility of the realm; and such can be ascribed only to the advantage of monopoly and the greatness of their profits. The merchants of London had acquired immense wealth as early as the reign of Edw. 3d, and not long after, Bristol could assert the riches of certain merchants, in no inferior competition.

Nor were these predatory acts confined to the merchants of the Mediterranean Sea. Piracy prevailed in the Baltic and the Icelandic Ocean, and

* *Fabyan's* Chronicle (reprint), p. 663. 36th Henry 6th.

even in the British Channel. Even the British ports, as Hull and Yarmouth, sent out marauders against London and Bristol.* In 1379 the King directed a writ for the punishment and fine before the Courts of Westminster, against certain merchants who had forcibly taken a ship belonging to William and John Canynges (the grandfather and father of our William) into Hartlepool, when on her voyage to Calais and Flanders.†

It will be readily surmised, that this constant risque to which navigation, in general, had become liable, rendered all the methods of defence, at that time practicable at sea, absolutely necessary.

In 1347, twenty two ships (naves guerrinæ) and 480 seamen were furnished by the trade of Bristol; and in the previous year twenty four ships and 608 men. These were impressed or hired, as they were eventually paid for, both for their use and wages. A few exceeded 200 tons burthen; but they were mostly from forty to one hundred. The larger, transported the treasures of the East to Italy, and sometimes to England. Some of them were purchased at Bristol for voyages to the Baltic, but the smaller were called Cogs, as the Marie-Cog; the Cog James and John, &c.; which denomination appears from a MS., in the possession of the late Charles Joseph Harford, Esq., and copied by my late highly esteemed friend Mr. Seyer, in his elaborate and valuable history of this City.

I have collected these facts from Anderson and

* *Rymer's* Fœdera, 1315.

† *Surties' Hist. of Durham.*

Macpherson, the two most able writers on the subject of British navigation and commerce.

The trade of Bristol continued to advance in extent and prosperity, until the reign of Henry 6th, the proper æra of William Canynges, who appears to have engrossed the traffic with the Genoese for stock-fish and the other merchandise of the Baltic, and with English woollens, in exchange for the produce of Italy and the Levant. There is a patent dated 1450, granted exclusively to him, in contravention to an existing act of parliament, to "load certain vessels of any burthen, with lawful merchandise to Iceland and Finland, for fish, during two years, excepting the merchandise of the staple of Calais," and in the preamble, it specifically states, that the King (Henry 6th) was under obligation to him, for great personal service.* This circumstance makes it evident, that he was not then a partisan of the Duke of York.

In 1461, when Edward 4th had taken possession of the Crown, he made a progress through the western parts of the kingdom for the purpose of levying a forced loan upon the mercantile cities, and remained, for some time, at Bristol.† Canynges was then Mayor, and as the King's escheator, had the management of it. The assessment was made according to the value and number of the vessels belonging to each merchant, individually. William Wyrcestre has preserved a list of Canynges' ships which requires some examination. That the

* *Rymer's* Fœdera. V. ii. 277. 1450.

† *Stowe's* Chron. 1461.

inscription with verses, and this list, were not placed over the tomb in Redcliff church, at that period, but in the reign of Elizabeth, no one, the least conversant, can doubt.*

This list enumerates nine ships—one of 900 tons —one of five, and two of four hundred tons, and likewise a vessel which was lost in Iceland of 160 tons. In 1480, Thomas Strange is stated to have possessed twelve ships, of which no farther particulars are given, but it is a proof, that Canynges' opulence was not singular.

That any ship of so large a burthen could have been received, at that time, into the Port of Bristol, may admit of doubt. I have been informed by an intelligent friend, that ships, in this account,

* This tomb, when erected by Canynges, was composed of plain carved freestone, and had no escocheon of his arms. Such being the three blackmoor's heads do not appear as attached to the architecture of any part of the church. It is presumed from satisfactory evidence, that W. Canynges never used these armorial bearings. In an ancient MS. of the arms borne by the several Lord Mayors of London, they are first attributed to his brother, Thomas Canynges. In the capital of a pillar we see W. Canynges' device, or merchant's mark, being a heart and the letters W. C. on either side, which are repeated once in a fragmented window of stained glass. In the reign of Elizabeth a fashion more generally prevailed of painting such monuments with various colours, when this was so deformed, and the arms thereon first emblazoned. The verses are much in the style of Thomas Churchyard, a very popular poet in that age, who was a known composer of Epitaphs. Canynges' seal has the rude figure of a Blackmoor's head only. He commonly used his merchant's mark.

said to have been of 360 tons, did not as to their actual burthen, exceed one half of their tonnage, at present. Ships, as now constructed, measuring 500 tons will, in fact, convey eight or nine hundred tons; whereas it is strictly probable, that, those belonging to Canynges would not have borne a burthen equal to that measurement. It is observed by Anderson, that "although the larger ships had English names, there is a doubt, whether we had ships of that size, of our own building. Canynges might have taken or purchased them from the Hanseatics, the Venetians, or Genoese, all of whom had ships of even a larger burthen, at that time." Stowe, in his history, calls these "great carriques of Jené" (Genoa.)

Not only the ships which were intended to convey armies into France, were differently constructed, but they afterward served to carry pilgrims to the shrine of St. James, at Compostella in Gallicia, the resort to which place was decided by the Pope, to be of equal virtue, with a voyage to Jerusalem itself. Some of those which were fitted out from Bristol, were capable of taking 200 persons in a single voyage, which to the merchants, was no unprofitable adventure. Persons of both sexes, and of all ranks, were urged to perform this holy duty, the fervour of which devotion prevailed chiefly during the reign of Henry 6th. We learn from W. Wyrcestre, that "Robert Sturmye, a merchant of Bristol, began his voyage to Jerusalem, in 1446, with 160 pilgrims, and that on his return he was shipwrecked at Modon, on the Greek coast, near Navarino, (which has been lately brought to our notice.) His ship, called the Cog-Anne, was dashed against a rock, and thirty-seven men were drowned; who were buried by the Bishop of Modon, who piously erected an oratory over them." As the art of navigation was progressively advancing, the ardour for discoveries in new and hitherto unknown regions, prevailed in every maritime nation of Europe; and these were directed to the vast Atlantic Ocean. This spirit animated the merchants of Bristol, but the earliest account we have of undertaking similar expeditions, has a date later, by six years, than Canynge's death. Wyrcestre informs us, "that in 1480, July 15th, the ship of John Jay, the younger, of 800 tons, and another, began their voyage from Kingroad to the island (the continent of Brasile) to the west of Ireland, ploughing their way through the sea....and Llyde was the pilot of the ships, the most scientific mariner in all England, (*scientificus marinarius totius Angliæ*); and news came to Bristol, on Monday, September 18 (1481), that the said ships sailed about the sea, during nine months, and did not find the island, but driven by tempests they returned to a port on the coast of Ireland for the repose of themselves and mariners."

This adventure from Bristol may claim precedence in point of date, before all others, as far as navigating the North Atlantic, and thus identifying the coast of Brasil. Columbus certainly had not seen it, in his voyage of 1474, when he discovered Hispaniola, &c. The real discovery which was confirmed by landing, was made by Martin Behem, of Nuremberg, then in the service of the King of

Portugal, in the year 1484. But in 1501, Columbus who made another voyage of discovery, and sailed round the whole coast of Brasil, was yet obliged to return to Portugal without having effected his purpose. Our own Sebastian Cabot after having discovered Newfoundland, made likewise an unsuccessful voyage to Brasil.

After, what may perhaps be considered as too long a digression, I will revert to the personal history of the subject of this memoir, and of his family and contemporaries. At the accession of Edward 4th, 1461, William Canynges was Mayor. That he was reconciled to the new government may be attributed to the influence of his half brother Thomas Young, who was burgess in parliament, and who was a zealous Yorkist.* The connection already mentioned with his family, was the primary cause of his subsequent prosperity. Wyrcestre says, that he paid the new King 3000 marks "pro pace suâ habendâ." This expression may admit of two meanings—either that it was an acquitance in the Exchequer for the merchants' general contribution, which as Mayor he was

* Thomas Young, Sergeant at law, Recorder, and afterwards a puisne Judge of the King's Bench. He proposed the regency of the Duke of York in Parliament. William Wyrcestre in his Annales Rerum Anglicarum printed in *Hearne's* Lib. Niger. p. 475.—" 1449. Hoc anno, in eodem parliamento, T. Yonge, Bristol' apprenticius in lege, movit quod quia Rex adhuc non habere prolem, quod esset securitas regno, ut aperte constaret quis esset hæres apparens? Et nominavit Ducem Eboraci. Quâ de causâ, idem Thomas fuit postea commissus turri Londoniæ."

bound to receive; or, that it was a fine imposed upon himself for his former attachment to the House of Lancaster.* He was included in the commission which condemned the brave Sir Baldwin Fulford (the *Sir Charles Bawdin* of *Chatterton*), which must have been to him a most painful duty. Bristol owes to him, the procuring from the King, a confirmation of former charters, and grants of farther liberties, which may have been partly purchased by the 3000 marks above mentioned. His prudent and beneficial conduct in the execution of his municipal offices appears on record.†

Of the merchants who nearly equalled him in wealth and influence, who bore the same part in the government of the town, and who, from the practice of monopolies, then prevalent, were engaged in most lucrative commerce, much genuine information is afforded by an examination of their wills. From these we learn satisfactorily, if not the extent of their wealth, the progress of domestic convenience by the introduction of many articles, at an earlier period than we had assigned to them; numerous utensils of silver, embossed plates and bowls, embroidered beds, apparel of rich materials with the most costly furs, are severally described as subjects of testamentary bequests. We must not then suppose, that such refinements were totally

* *Stowe*, p. 416. The Commissioners appointed for this trial were Henry Bourchier Earl of Essex, Sir William Hastyngs, Knt., Richard Choke, a judge, and William Canynges, Mayor.

† Bristol Charters, 1 Edw. 4. 1461, No. 21, *Seyer's* Edition.

strange to the rich man of the middle centuries; or that we now possess luxury unknown before. We have varied the mode only, not the effect.

If Canynges possessed the highest rank, in point of wealth and civil importance, at the zenith of his prosperity; others there were, whose opulence and mercantile concerns, were scarcely inferior to his own.* The names of Young, Frampton, Derby, Spelly, Shipward and Strange, and especially Sturmye, not unfrequently occur in the magisterial lists of that time. Of the last mentioned, Wyrcestre reports his remarkable hospitality. "He built the cloth hall, and a large dwelling-house near it, in which this venerable merchant kept an ample and open table, as well for foreigners, as other gentlemen."

In the wills of these persons, which are still to be inspected, we perceive the nature and description of their wealth, with the apparel, armour, plate and furniture, then most valued, and the particular employment of their ships. In these too, are described certain domestic customs, and the internal arrangement of their dwelling houses; and moreover, injunctions are recited against second marriages,† avowed or secret, which are to be punished with a degree of severity, accordant with the rigid maxims of those times.

* The wills of several individuals of these families are preserved in the Corporation Archives, all of which give evidence of their ample wealth.

† Wills of Walter Derby 1385, and of Walter Frampton 1388.

Their costly bequests of vestments and missals* to churches and chantries, with the multitudinous attendants of priests and servants at their funeral obsequies, were provided for, by a very large expenditure, and an ample distribution to the poor. As being aware that several sumptuary laws were then in effect, we are surprised to find such hoards of magnificent apparel, specially divided among children and friends. Although Canynges' church of Redcliff so far exceeded any other in Bristol, yet it had not the priority, for Derby and Frampton, in their lifetime also, had erected the churches of St. Werburg and St. John.

The trade of importing wine from Gascony and Spain, was conducted in a peculiar manner; and was then engrossed by one or two of the merchants above mentioned. Their ships were furnished with casks of very great measure and guarded with vast hoops of iron, and were indeed a part of the ship itself. These are distinctly enumerated in their wills, in barbarous latin, "Item, lego viginti pipas-gardæ," meaning pipes bound with iron. There was likewise a fraternity of wine-halliers and porters, to whom large sums were given at their masters' funeral dole.

About this period, and indeed earlier, the mer-

* The bequests of vestments and missals are most remarkable and extensive in the wills of John Shipward 1473, to St. Stephen's church, and of W. Canynges 1474, to Redcliff. In the same year "William Coder "lego omnes meos libros Latinales Johanni Coder, consanguineo meo in custodiâ suâ, necnon omnes meos libros latinales existentes in cistâ infra domum meam, cum dictâ cistâ."

chants were spaciously, if not splendidly lodged. Wyrcestre speaks of several of these large mansions. Olyver, the Recorder, had built one, opposite to St. Peter's church, and Norton another behind it. Vyel and Bagod had rebuilt and enlarged towers in the Town-wall, and added dwelling-houses to them. In Small-street, there still remains a front of handsome architecture towards a court. We may well imagine, that the subject of this memoir would feel a similar ambition of exhibiting his wealth. Accordingly, we are informed, that one of superior dimensions and certain architectural beauty, was erected by him, above the river Avon, and fronting the street, to which it extended. It presented the form of a tower. Our topographer describes it as "mansio pulcherrima," having four bay windows with chambers built "ornatissimo modo"—in the best style of architecture. The dimensions were twenty yards by sixteen. This part of the edifice can be marked out no longer, with any satisfaction; but the hall with its finely carved roof still remains, though its interior has been materially changed by subsequent alterations; as it appears to have been used as an oratory or chapel, probably for the Catholic service. Of this mansion-house Canynges himself bears testimony. In his will he bequeaths it, with other tenements, to Elizabeth, the widow of his son William.* Upon her second marriage with John Depeden, Esq., J. Twinyhow, the Recorder, was her trustee, who released to them

* From Deeds in Mr. Cumberland's possession.

fifty-five messuages, sixteen gardens, &c., in Bristol for her life, with remainder to Thomas her son, one of which was the house "in quo W. C. Mercator dudum inhabitavit.* In 1484, Thomas Canynges sold it; and in 1500 it was the residence of Thomas Brooke, the father of John Brooke, whose tomb, inlaid with brass figures, is seen in Redcliff church. It was then called "Canynge's place." These notices, if of any other house, might not be required here.

No other of his contemporary merchants possessed so large a rental of messuages, gardens and orchards, within the walls, as William Canynges. In point of number, if those which he inherited from his ancestors or had himself acquired were accurately reckoned up, from the several deeds and wills they would amount to scarcely less than one hundred. This great property is the more remarkable, because many others were possessed by ecclesiastics, as chantry priests. There were fifteen convents, who were possessed severally of houses in Bristol, and some were part of the Royal demesnes. In order to communicate some idea of the nature of the great property above recited, I will venture upon a description.

An ancient tenement or house, during the middle centuries as inhabited by the "Burgesses of Bristow" was thus constructed. The souterrain was a very large cellar (*cellarium*), for the reception of large and heavy articles of merchandise, with a groined and ribbed roof of stone, or else covered

* From Deeds in Mr. Cumberland's possession.

with beams of timber extending under the street, and divided by arches and pillars; but these were less frequent. They are said to have amounted to 169 within the walls.

The ground floor was partitioned into narrow shops (*shopæ*), three or four under the same roof, with stalls or bulk heads, and open to the street. They served for the daily traffic; and in the merchants' houses, a hall (*Aula*) was built behind them, having a high-arched roof of timber-frame. The first floor contained the habitable house (*Camera*), bedroom, parlour (*Parlatorium*), and the kitchen (*Coquina*), all of which are recited in deeds and wills. And lastly garrets (*Solaria*), which had two projecting stories under the roof.

Uniformity of plan pervaded the more spacious mansions. They were, in general, constructed of oak or chesnut timber frame, with projecting brackets grotesquely carved at the ends, as were the door-cases. Bay windows were attached to each story, and even the intermediate wall was filled with glass. So essential was the comfort of light and air to this dense habitation to those

"Long in populous cities pent."

Modern improvement has laid most of these low, and without remains.

The unconscious simplicity by which in these personal documents the manners and opinions of contemporary individuals are discovered, present to us a natural picture, which conjectural delineation cannot imitate. Imagination from the stores of information already accumulated in the mind, and the impulse of a feeling congenial with antiquarian pursuits may describe, happily, scenes and manners as they appeared to have subsisted, during any of the periods, which are called the "Middle Ages." But let us not undervalue genuine notices of men and things, transmitted to us by those who were witnesses conversant with minute transactions peculiar to their age, as they were really seen with their own eyes, and which when they noted them down, they were heedless should ever have reached the present day. Shall we not prefer the rude, and sometimes confused, sketches of William Wyrcestre, as lovers of genuine topography, to the vague traditions which are perpetuated by indiscriminating antiquaries? Shall we allow his occasional discrepancies to invalidate his whole authority?

Of Canynge's own family I shall now subjoin a brief account, with respect to his immediate descendants. It appears that he married early in life; but the surname of his wife is not known. There is a curious tradition concerning her, which I shall notice. She died about 1460, when the monument with effigies was placed in Redcliff church by her husband, as a memorial of her, and of himself. Their children were William and John, both of whom deceased before their father. No mention occurs of any daughter, William married Isabel or Elizabeth,* daughter and heir of John Vowel, Esquire, of Wells. She had a large jointure from her inherited property and from the settlement and bequest of her father-in-law, having remarried John Depeden, Esquire, of Bristol, by

* From Deeds in Mr. Cumberland's possession.

whom she left no issue. By her first husband she had two sons, Thomas and William, and one daughter Agnes. Of Thomas I have discovered no farther than that he was of age in 1484, if not earlier, when he sold " Canynge's Place." This alienation was disputed in Chancery, by William Spenser, the Executor, and the Chantry priests of Redcliff, but confirmed. No mention is made of this elder son in William Canynge's will, and most probably because he inherited the estate of his mother, at Wells. The other son William and the daughter Agnes both died minors; a fact certainly known, by the lapse of the Bristol property, which had been devised to them and their heirs, into the hands of William Spenser the Mayor, the Corporation, and the Chantry priests of Redcliff. John, the other son of W. Canynges, left a widow, but no children. Both these widows were endowed in his will.

Thus, we may attribute to a probable and rational cause, the resolution which he took of abandoning the cares of a busy mercantile life, of which the chief consolation and support had failed him, by the premature death of his two sons.

From his earliest youth, he was deeply imbued with religious feeling, and was a faithful and zealous follower of the church of Rome, which was then prevalent in this country. His friend and confessor from his earliest youth was John Carpenter, born at Westbury upon Trim, and who eventually became bishop of Worcester; and these impressions were fostered by him. He, it was, who probably suggested the rebuilding of Redcliff church, upon so grand a scale, for he was a known patron of ecclesiastical architecture. He greatly contributed, if he were not the designer of St. Mary's church at Oxford ; where his statue is seen in one of the niches of the tower; and he rebuilt the College at Westbury upon Trim.

Canynges gave certain demonstration of his piety. In 1465, he became a benefactor to the Franciscan Friars, for his name with that of others to be inserted in a yearly mass, paying them "a quarter of an ox value forty pence—of a sheep value sixteen pence, and forty pence in parvâ pecuniâ, in small change, to be distributed among the poor, in bread and beer."*

In 1467, he gave to repair the tenements, then dilapidated, which belonged to two chantries in Redcliff church, heretofore founded by Everard Le Franceys ; and to found another to be called "W. Canynges' priest," the sum of £340 by a deed in Mr. Cumberland's collection ;† and not £500 as misstated. In the next year, he obtained from King Edward 4th a patent to establish two priests, for a daily mass before the altar of St. George, with a salary of nine marks, and a chamber for each. He had previously erected a building to receive all these, near the churchyard.‡ Wyrcestre speaks of this edifice, as having bay windows, probably on the plan of those built for the Vicar's choral of Wells, by Bishop Beckington, about the same time.

* Original deeds.

† Original deeds.

‡ Itin. W. Wyrcestre, p. 84.

But Canynges' munificent mind, under holy influences, meditated the consummation of a work, which should ensure the respect of ages. The most ostensible piety at that period was the enhancing the grandeur and beauty of the House of God.

The parochial church of St. Mary Redcliff has been justly considered as the wonder of western England. Its great space, its accurate dimensions, and its elaborate architecture, have, upon fair comparison, intitled it to that singular praise. A circumstance, which has much enhanced this admiration, has been the report that it sprang from the munificence and perseverance of one benefactor. Let this fact be examined by adducing the best evidence, and that claim may be made subject to certain abatement. If to investigate truth be, in some instances, to lessen traditional fame which has descended to our times, without examination, the present age is become more interested in discovering realities ; and in detaching such errours from seeming authorities, which have never been submitted to the test of historic proof.

It has not been recollected by all, that there have been *three* distinct structures dedicated to St. Mary, erected in successive centuries, upon the sacred spot, from its elevation above the Avon, and the colour of the soil, denominated "The Red Cliff." The first chapel was not built before the reign of Henry 3d. It was founded by contribution, oblations for indulgences, and legacies of those who had newly inhabited Redcliff-street, as the feudal tenants of the Lords Berkeley, in right of their great manor of Bedminster. "The men of Red Clive" as they were then called, were of considerable opulence, for they contributed 1000 marks to King John in 1210, a sum equal to that paid by the whole town of Bristol. Robert, the second Baron Berkeley of that name, gave by deed a spring for the supply of a fountain, to the church, in 1232; and of the same date, is an indulgence for thirty days from John Bishop of Limerick, to all who should give to the carrying on of that building.* Several similar documents occur among those in Mr. Cumberland's possession. Other Bishops in Ireland had made like concessions of pardon, for that purpose. About the same period, a very considerable trade and intercourse subsisted between Bristol and Dublin, with other ports upon that coast, the seigniory of which had been conferred upon the first mentioned town, by a charter of Henry the Second. No proof is known, that this first structure was more than a small chapel, and it has been asserted in errour, that it was identified with the chapel dedicated to the Holy Ghost, called, in vernacular language, "St. Sprites."

As wealth increased, and piety became more influential over property, the merchants of Redcliff determined to re-edify their church, or at least to extend it, upon a large scale. A very opulent family, called probably from their origin Le Franshe and Fraunceys, and those of De Burton and De la Riviere were the chief merchants who inhabited

* Licence from David Kelly, Archbishop of Cashel, 1238, and from John Bishop of Limerick, 1232. Cumberland MSS.

Redcliff-street, at the commencement of the fourteenth century. These families collectively, were the early benefactors; who were enumerated in the bede-rolls of three several chantries, founded by them in this second church. Nothing that I have hitherto seen tends to evidence that Simon de Burton was the sole founder of the original, church, if he then lived; for the date of his mayoralty is at least sixty years subsequently to it. But the building of the second has been attributed in some scattered MSS. to William Canynges, the elder. Now, I have proved by his will and likewise that of his son John, that they were both, at that period, manufacturers and cloth-merchants in Touker-street; and that they then possessed a small tenement only in Redcliff; whilst Frauncеys, Burton, De la Riviere, and Young possessed it almost entirely. They had founded chantries in the new edifice, and the tomb of Everard le Franshe is still seen there; but William Canynges leaves only twenty shillings as a customary dole to the vicar. Is it probable that if he had built the church, he would have so poorly remunerated its minister?

According to this view, which is confirmed by several existing documents, the following is the true arrangement of the dates of the erection of the two first churches.

The earliest notice that the first church was in progress of building has been already specified. It is more probable, that it had been found too small, from the great increase of inhabitants in that quarter, than that it should have required a reconstruction from decay. I consider that the square or interior of the great north porch is a part, and perhaps the only remaining part of it. Decisive evidence fixes the commencement of the second church to the last ten years of the fourteenth century. Its progress was necessarily slow, not only from the magnitude of the work, especially of the tower and spire, but also from the gradual supply of funds sufficiently ample to conduct such an undertaking to its final close. That event had certainly taken place in 1446, when by a tremendous tempest the spire was precipitated upon the nave and south aisle, and entirely overwhelmed them. The Choir and Transepts received only a partial and reparable injury. Nor can it be supposed that the roofs of parts distant from the Tower at the west end, could have suffered demolition. Armorial bearings of Stafford, Berkeley, Beauchamp, and Montacute, still carved in the groined roof of stone, in the north transept, afford no inconsiderable proof of the contrary. But the style of architecture leaves no reasonable doubt, if compared with that of the nave, after it had been rebuilt.

The exangular Porch has equal singularity and beauty of construction, and I do not recollect its parallel in England, if the west door of Litchfield cathedral be not one; but the style prevailed in Normandy, at Rouen, in the porches of the Cathedral and that of St. Maclou, with strong analogy at least; and about the period of its erection. This remark applies no less to the porch of the western front. Of these, the remarkable feature is the ogee arch, and mouldings richly filled with matted foliage, consisting of leaves and flowers; the middle one having a tracery of conjoined lozenges, which inclose small sculptures. The tall external niches, now mostly vacant, contained effigies, said to have been of royal personages.

The ornament of sunk quaterfoils in the frames of the windows of the Choir or Chancel, exactly resemble those of Litchfield cathedral, which are there placed upon the jambs only, in the fourteenth century. It is of rare occurrence; while the sharp angular heads of those in the chapel beyond, are not earlier than 1450. The Oratories in Redcliff church were built to receive perpetual chantries. There were likewise four altars, two dedicated to St. Blase and St. Nicholas, and two more to St. Katherine and St. George, with their attendant priests, whose office was to offer orisons for the dead and the living by name. To mention these in detail, may appear to be irrelevant, because the public have long since forgotten to respect them; and the property by which they were sustained, has passed to more beneficial purposes. But in a philosophical view, such motives and opinions are not deprived of their just value, because they were in fact created and indelibly fixed in the mind, by the predominant circumstances of those early times. Historical accuracy will now give to them a certain degree of importance. From its very favourable site, the tower acquires a commanding elevation, greater than might have been expected from its massiveness—the internal diameter being 24 feet by 22, and the walls seven feet thick—the height, independently of the fractured spire, 120 feet. All its parts and ornamental details are large and majestic. For the present singular termination of the spire, modern improvers are not accountable, for it was certainly the work of Canynges' architect, and probably the last; for it appears to have been only an expedient.* It was then called the "corona" or "garlond," a termination not unusual on the continent. To those who are interested in the history of bells, it may be curious information, to know that no tower in England contained a peal so heavy and sonorous, neither at that time, nor since. Wyrcestre has particularised them.† They were six only, of which the heaviest was seven thousand and twenty-four pounds avoirdupoise, and the least, thirteen hundred. The great bell at Gloucester, which is still heard, is twenty-four pounds lighter, and comparison affords a sure test.

I may presume to hazard the patiencc of the audience by condensing the minute statement, which respects the subordinate parts of this magnificent pile, as it is given by William Wyrcestre, not upon his own authority, but specifically from the information of Norton, the master mason,‡ perhaps the architect, employed in these great works; and such an authority must plead for its introduction with the amateurs of what has been called Gothic architecture now present. Certain

* W. W. p. 105. "et latitudo de la garlond xi. pedes."

† W. W. p. 133.

‡ W. W. p. 133, "per relationem—Norton Magister (Master Mason), ecclesiæ de Redcliff."

it is, that the few extracts hitherto made from it have been garbled and partially misunderstood.

With respect to the exterior, he has the following observations :—* "The parish church of St. Mary Redcliff is situate upon a high hill, built like a cathedral, with a large square tower containing bells of very great weight. The diameter of the bell-tower, with its vaulted ceiling, newly made, is twenty-four feet from east to west, and twenty-three from north to south. The base of the square upon which the spire was placed, consists of eight pannels; and the first part of it is composed of cemented stones of two feet in thickness, and is so continued lessening to a certain height, and from thence there are four sconces issuing from the angles as a bond of the spire. This spire, not long since, stood one hundred feet high. The elevation of the tower is one hundred and twenty feet, to the springing of the spire, and with it, now broken, reaches to two hundred feet, the whole being three hundred from the lowest foundation, and the platform of the fragmented part is sixteen feet across, and eleven within the 'garlond' or balustrade. Every stone at the base of the spire, is two feet in thickness; but on its present summit only eight inches. The walls immediately above the foundation are seven feet thick. There are sixteen large buttresses, beside those of the tower, on the north; and twenty-five on the south; some of which are two yards lower than the parapet. The whole external length is two hundred and thirty-one feet.

* W. W., 157, 158.

"The circumference of the chapel of St. Mary, in the great porch, with the images of kings, curiously sculptured in freestone, together with the door-case, skilfully wrought, is forty-four yards. The dimension of the western door, which is most artificially finished in freemason's work, is seven feet and nine to the centre." Norton's description of every particle which composes it, is then minutely given, in terms of masonry, then in common usage, and still to be explained. A more scientific detail of any other church is not found. He is not less circumstantial as to the interior elevation of the fabrick.*

"The length of the South porch is seven yards, and the breadth four and a half. That of the three aisles (meaning the nave and aisles) is fourteen yards, and the intercolumniation of each ten feet. In the transept, there are eight arches from north to south. In every window of the Clerestory, each of which is five feet broad, there are five glazed divisions, and in the windows at each end three. The principal pillar of the four, which support the tower, at the west end of the nave, has one hundred and three "bowtels" (that is, perpendicular mouldings), which surround the shafts, and the circumference of each pillar is six yards, whilst that of the others is four only. The height of the arched vault which covers the whole fabrick, the nave, two aisles, and transept, is eighty steps, computing the number of those which go to the roof of timber frame and lead; as a plumber told me on the eighth of September, 1480, each

* Norton's statement condensed and translated, pp. 158, &c.

step containing eight inches at least, so that the whole height of the vault to its centre, is fifty-three feet four inches, and the length of the nave with the choir, one hundred and thirteen paces (about twenty inches each); of the transept sixty-seven paces; and of our Lady's chapel sixteen yards. The width of the transept, including the space between the nave and choir, is thirty-six yards, and the total length is sixty-seven."

Will any professional architect, or amateur of architecture, take these measurements in his hand, and compare them with an edifice, which remains the same from Wyrcestre's time, and will he discover discrepancies, which ought fairly speaking, to invalidate the whole scale? I assert, with diffidence, that such will not be the result. Because my old and venerated topographer had amused himself after the turmoils of a busy life, in which he was engaged, and which was spent in many important transactions, during the reigns both of the fifth and sixth Henry, and has left a mass of notices respecting his native and beloved town, with repetition and uncertainty, indeed, in some instances, when correction was interrupted by the lassitude of age, or the hand of death. Shall we repudiate with the fastidiousness of modern advancement in knowledge, as useless and unworthy of acceptation, simple descriptions; and prefer unauthorised tradition or conjecture merely for that they have been reiterated?

The prevailing style is that which has been denominated by Mr. Rickman, with geometrical propriety, the "Perpendicular," because the mouldings, and the panelling by which the additions or restorations made by Canynges are pervaded, have universally an upright direction.

It has been allowed, by those who are most extensively informed on the subject of the architecture of the middle ages, that this church displays one of the most spacious and complete examples of the later style. Other large parochial churches of the same æra, as at Coventry and St. Edmundsbury, offer not an equal competition. Had these been strictly copied by the architects of the numerous churches, lately erected at the national expense, instead of their having adopted parts, perfect in themselves, but capriciously assorted and combined, we should not so often see "Gothic in masquerade."

Two circumstances of privation have contributed to an extent almost destructive of the original and nearly supernatural effect of a Gothic church. They are the total occupation of the floor by pews, which present unconquerable obstructions; and the substitution of raw glass in the windows, for the holy glow of prismatical colours. What is now left to exalt the imagination, and to feed the fervour of religious feeling, heightened, as it then was, by perceptible objects? It is the admirable skill of the architect—the commanding symmetry or the vast mass of a structure raised by human labour, and perfected by the ingenuity of man. That surely remains to astonish modern eyes, although the illusion be departed, never to return by any imitation of those stupendous efforts of labour and of skill.

All who entertain a genuine love of investigation, will regret that any sufficient evidence of the expense incurred in this building, or to whom the architecture of so remarkable a church is decidedly due, has eluded no careless research. The restorer himself, in the time spent of pious humility, never alludes to this sumptuous work in his will, or in any document that I have seen, that only excepted respecting the monument which he erected for himself and wife, soon after her death, "in loco quam construi et feci in parte australi ejusdem ecclesiæ," meaning the southern transept.

Norton, whose Christian name is not specified, was the master mason, and in most instances that term was synonimous with architect. If anywhere, the "computus," or roll of expenses, for the current year, was deposited in that mysterious chest, "Cista Wilhelmi Canynges," so recognised and preserved in the muniment room of Redcliff church, but which, with several others, has been utterly despoiled.* Wyrcestre seems to fix the time occupied in building to eight years; and states that one hundred artificers were employed daily, which is extremely probable.† Analogy is the only scale by which any judgment can be formed as to the actual cost. In the same century, King Henry 6th had allotted rents of £1000 a year to

* Such strong chests did not contain deeds and writings only, but a stock of money, several of which still remain in the more ancient Colleges of Oxford and Cambridge.

† W. W. p. 114. "Exhibuit per octo annos, 800 homines in navibus occupatos; et habuit operarios et carpentarios, masons, &c., omni die, 100 homines."

build King's College Chapel at Cambridge. Edward 4th allowed more for Windsor Chapel, and Henry 7th at Westminster expended £14,000. We cannot estimate Redcliff church at less than these; and if this computation be just, £40,000 of the present value of money would scarcely complete it.

In 1468, having completed his original intention, urged, as I have before suggested, by Bishop Carpenter, the loss of both his sons, and the consideration that minors only would inherit his wealth at a distant period, he resolved to dedicate the remnant of his days to the service of God and the church. He was ordained Accolyte Sept. 19, 1467; Deacon and Priest April 16, 1468; and was then appointed the first Dean of the Benedictine College of Westbury, then newly modelled by his friend. In this retreat he passed the last six years of his life. He had procured, according to a practice then not unusual, his effigy as a priest, to be carved and placed as a monument in the chapel there, and with a remarkable figure at his feet of an old man, apparently in an agony, embodying a metaphysical idea of putting off the old man, from his having abandoned his lay character. This was intended as a daily incitement of his piety. When Westbury college was burned down by Prince Rupert's army in 1643, to prevent the Parliament's army from taking possession of it, upon their surrender of Bristol, this monument was saved, and is now in Redcliff church.

Canynges' will* bears date Nov. 12, 1474, at

* Canynges's will, dated Nov. 12, 1474, is extant in the Register Office, Doctors Commons, London. "Regist. Wattis quatern." 18, Fol. 125.

From Canynge's Monument:
in Redcliff Church.

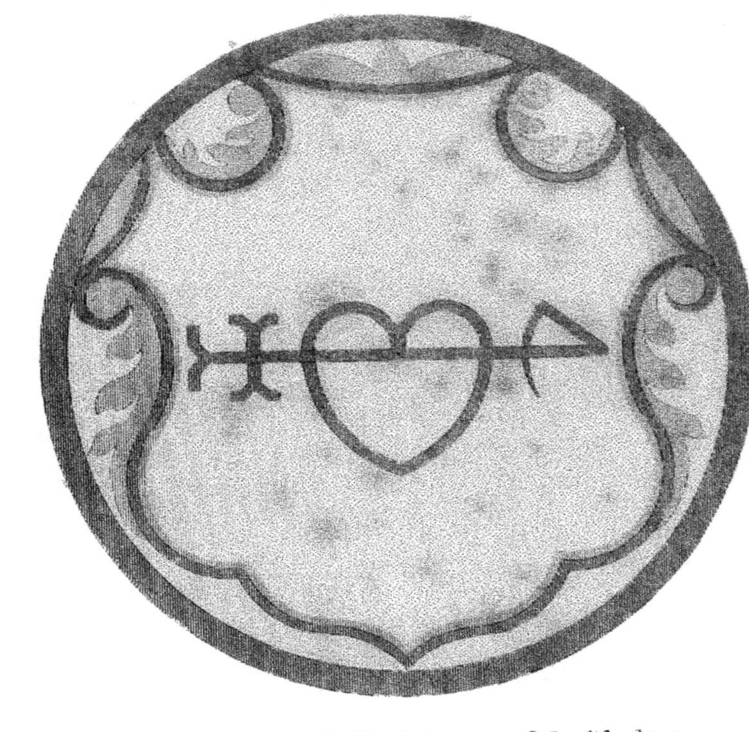

Circle of Stain'd Glass in one of the Windows
of Redcliff Church.

Westbury, and he died early in the next year, aged conjecturally 74 years. His funeral was conducted to his place of sepulture in Redcliff church, accompanied by a large concourse of ecclesiastics, particularly of the mendicant orders, within the town, to whom he had bequeathed legacies of an amount very unusual in those days.

Useless as the endeavour might be to discover the origin of two silly traditions respecting Canynges, it may gratify our love of truth to controvert them. One is, that he was commanded by Edward 4th to marry some lady of the court, and that he became a priest in order to avoid so incongruous a connection at his advanced period of life.* The other, which seems more worthy notice, is, that his wife had unfairly possessed herself of the grand secret of the Elixir of life, and that such was the real source of her husband's wonderful wealth. Some amusement may result from examining the latter of these extraordinary assertions, at least by allowable conjecture.

Whilst the mind of man remained in willing slavery to superstition, as to what regards a future state, it was prepared for the reception of such a fallacy as the philosopher's stone, or the transmutation of metals, which had been assumed by certain alchymists as the means of procuring in this life longevity without decay of health, and

* This lady might have been Katherine, the natural daughter of Anthony Wydeville, Earl Rivers, brother of the Queen, then so young as to render this tradition improbable. She was afterwards married to Sir Robert Poyntz, Knt.

riches without limit or exhaustion. So fascinating was this expectation, that even the wise and potent King Edward 3d became a memorable dupe to the specious promises of Raymond Lully; and the weak Henry 6th granted patents to alchymists, who were to supply him with money to pay his army.*

Thomas Norton,† a native priest of Bristol, pretended to possess this invaluable secret, and became renowned for his skill in the occult science. But Pitts, his biographer, says, that having deceived many, he became at last a dupe himself, and died neglected and poor. After Canynges' death he compiled (1477) a didactic poem, called "The Ordinal," which was first printed in Ashmole's "Theatrum Chymicum," published in 1652. He thus speaks of himself—

"Thomas Norton, of Brisêtowe,
A perfect master ye may him trowe."

* Rymer's Fœd. v. 4, p. 384. The King (Edward 3d), understanding that John Rous and master W. of Dalby, made silver, &c., ordered them to bring their instruments before him. Rymer's Fœd. Rot Pat. 42. Hen. 6th. "Johanni Coble quod per artem Philosophiæ posset metalla imperfecta de proprio suo genere transferre et ea in aurum sive argentum transubstantiare." Similar patents had been granted 34 and 35 of his reign.

† Norton is styled by Bale "Alchymista sui temporis peritissimus." He finished his MS. in 1477, and says at the conclusion that he began to compile it when 28 years old—

"To the intent that men may beware thereby,
And for no other cause truly."

The title was "Crede mihi, seu-Ordinale."

"I made the elixir of lyfe,
Which me berefte a merchant's wyfe;
The Quintessence I made also,
With other secrets, many moe,
Which sinful people took me fro."

Ashmole, in a note, asserts that this merchant was Canynges, but offers not even the authority of tradition, much less of proof.*

It was necessary to quote these wretched rhymes, to shew what is the description of poets who flourished in this place, at the very same time with the imaginary Rowley. Who can discover any similarity in these effusions to the sublime "Song to Ælla?"

Norton was a charlatan, who, according to his own account, did not keep his secret like others, but was imprudently communicative, if indeed he had anything to discover.

The names of Canynges and Rowley have been of late so nearly associated in a popular fiction, that even in this slight essay, that circumstance cannot be entirely omitted without animadversion.

Thomas Chatterton, the real author of it, was a meteor in the Bristol hemisphere, which flitted, for a short moment, among its fixed stars. The prodigious precocity of his genius will not cease to excite surprise and admiration, from the extreme rarity of the occurrence—"ostendunt tantum fata" —whilst the sad event of his life will awaken a melancholy reflection of great talents, given indeed, but applied to no purposes of utility to mankind.

* See likewise Fuller's Worthies, who has the same story, with others as extraordinary.

After this endeavour to offer a true portrait of William Canynges, let us examine the travestied character of him, as exhibited by Chatterton.*

He is described as a poet and an epigrammatist, but the specimens given are certainly not happy. He is not only a writer of prologues, but an actor in a drama. Such freakish avocations but ill assort with the position which Canynges held in society. But these were the puerile inventions of this inconsiderate boy, who, even in the fabrication, betrayed his intention by a total contempt of verisimilitude, either in point of character or circumstance.

The late T. Warton, whose opinion has been now generally adopted, makes this observation, which is consonant to his known talent of discrimination. "Criticism, the companion and the assistant of truth, has endeavoured to replace those laurels on his head which he tore from his brow with his own hand."†

I now close these discussions, not without an apprehension that they may have been carried to too great a length—but, from old times, prolixity has been the privilege of an antiquary.

J. D.

April, 1831.

* Chatterton's Works, 3 vols. 8vo. Edited by Southey.

† Warton's Enquiry into the authenticity of the Poems attributed to Thomas Rowley. 8vo. p. 109.

INDEX.

A

B

C

D

E

F

G

M

N

O

T

U V

W

Y

PRINTED AT THE BRISTOL MIRROR OFFICE BY JOHN TAYLOR.